13 Training Schedules for Triathlons

Carlos Civit

authorHOUSE®

AuthorHouse™
1663 Liberty Drive
Bloomington, IN 47403
www.authorhouse.com
Phone: 1-800-839-8640

First published by AuthorHouse 3/16/2011

ISBN: 978-1-4567-2297-5 (e)
ISBN: 978-1-4567-2298-2 (hc)
ISBN: 978-1-4567-2299-9 (sc)

Library of Congress Control Number: 2010919575

Printed in the United States of America

Contents

PRE FACE:

Why did I decide to write a book about triathlons? The answer becomes obvious when you begin to surf on-line, conduct research in a library, peruse various magazines, or search the shelves of a local bookstore. While you may find plenty of information about triathlons, including training methods, history of the sport, specific triathlons accommodating various skill levels, what I have learned and what I would like to illustrate in this book, has not yet been published.

Throughout the years that I have been involved in triathlons or any endurance sport, I read many books and specialized magazines about the particular subject for which I trained. I competed and trained with hundreds of athletes, from beginners to world-class, with whom I shared opinions, experiences and mindsets about training. I noticed all of them, including myself, had the desire to know more about training about how to get faster, fitter, and all the "secrets" of those who perform at their highest individual levels, at professional levels, or just at levels indicative of Age Groupers. I noticed too, that a huge cross-section of the population that practices this sport would like to truly understand more about training methods, swim techniques, bikes and components, running drills and form, nutrition and supplements, and especially about how much truth is in all that has been suggested in published texts. In other words, what REALLY works and what doesn't. Blindly, we follow what has worked for others, what is in fashion, in season, or what professionals with credentials say and do.

It seems to me that when athletes are looking for answers to the questions above, especially questions connected to training, the answers are not just complex, but difficult to translate in terms of practical understanding.

Having said that, some find the information presented; impossible to apply to individual needs in a training schedule format.

In answer to these questions, "13 Training Plans for Triathlons" focuses in great detail on specific day-to-day trainings during 10 training weeks prior to your event.

Finally, this book reveals secrets about what has worked for athletes, like you, who want to perform at the highest level.

Chapter 1: UNDERSTANDING TRIATHLONS

If you are reading this book, you probably know what a triathlon is, its origins and its modern formats, from the well-known Sprint Distance, (750m swim + T1 + 20kms bike ride + T2 + 5kms run), to the Olympic Distance also known as the International Distance (1500m swim+ T1 + 40kms bike ride + T2 + 10kms run) , to the ½ Ironman distance (1900m swim+ T1 + 90kms bike ride + T2 + 21.1kms run) , to the "beast"; the Ironman (3.8km swim+ T1 + 180kms bike ride + T2 + 42.1kms run). Also worth mentioning are the triathlons with ITU format, or better known as drafting allowed races, and those where drafting is sanctioned with a Stop and go and 3' or 4' forced to rest at the T2 (bike/run transition) area. Actually, in this ever-growing worldwide sport, we find all kinds of distances, profiles, sizes, and formats, all with a common characteristic; you need to swim, bike and run at some point during the event.

Perhaps you are looking for help in your training. Possibly "how" or "when" to train involving key elements others have found useful and with which you may be able to identify. But before you start, there is something that must be mentioned.

There are only so many hours in a day that usually need to be arranged around school, work, family and the daily chores. It is necessary, therefore, to design a program that is specific to your needs (competitive or otherwise), and in many cases, will be personal and not transferable. Thus, total application of information of training plans found in this book, or any other source may not fit completely with your needs and may be difficult for the athlete to follow it to the letter. Nevertheless, the intent of this book is far from it.

Chapter 2: MAKE A PLAN AND SET REALISTICS SPECTATIONS

Did you ever notice that when you ask other athletes or friends about how they feel after their race, in a 90% of the cases you will get answers such as: "I had a bad race", " I only did it as a training day", "I met a friend during the race, we finished together" "I have an injury that is still bothering me" " I didn't train at all for the last few weeks," " I did a really long workout yesterday, and still feeling it", etc, etc. What is it about the human convention that we seem to come up with a multitude of excuses?

Many athletes put a lot of effort into training without carefully setting both a program and a goal. How fast do I want to race? How well can I perform? What is my real expectation, not only competing, but also training? So many times I hear "this is what I need to do", and then witness athletes failing over and over, trying to follow an unrealistic program. There is a huge difference between what needs to be done in order to accomplish a certain time or race performance, and what we truly physically are capable of. Not only because we may have our own physical limitations, but it may also happen that our lifestyles, won't allow us to perform as well as we really could do in a perfect situation. So we need to start being honest with ourselves. You may tell yourself you want to do an Ironman Distance, but you must also ask yourself whether it is possible given your specific lifestyle. Some other questions you may want to ponder are: Should my goal be for a shorter race that requires less training hours? Do I have responsibilities connected with family, business, job? Do I have a stressful life? Am I single, with a huge amount of free time?

Once you make the decision about the distance for which you want to train, there is another critical question to answer: How fast? Even though this is one of those questions that can only be answered after several weeks of specific training, it is also true, that to chose a certain path you need to know where to start from. As a trainer, I insist on clarity to the questions posed above so that we can develop a realistic training plan. In my first meeting with the athlete, I have noticed that almost 1 out of 2 seniors or advanced Age Groupers explain how good they used to be in his/her earlier sport career years, how fast they ran their best marathon, how fast they used to swim competitively at college, or even explain their battles on the weekend bike races. But, is it realistic to think that if you once were a fantastic athlete, you can be again? Is it realistic to think that if you once ran a marathon in 3 hours you are going to run that fast in a Triathlon? Well, that is a complex question, with a more difficult answer. Normally my experience tells me that it is hard for the majority of us to accomplish the same performance today that we accomplished in our glory days, based on 98% of the cases being attributed to lifestyle rather than capabilities. Because of this percentage rate, we must first be honest with ourselves and start just below our expectations. We always have time to modify the training, increasing our stamina and morale with each step we take.

2.1 HOW GOOD COULD I EXPECT TO BE AND HOW LONG WILL IT TAKE ME?

Generally, it takes at least 5 years without interruption of well-planned training to peak in your sport. From that point, improvement will probably occur, but in smaller increments.

I once had a chat with one of my colleagues, and we came to the conclusion that some of the variables that influence your peak performance are as follows:

1. Talent
2. Physical Type of Body
3. Training.
4. Commitment
5. Knowledge and Experience in the Sport.
6. Environment

Carlos Civit

Chapter 3: TALENT

In my earlier years as a cyclist, I remember well two of my training buddies, both with incredible talent for the sport, but in two totally different ways. I remember David Reartes, 2 overall in the Catalunya cyclocross championship and team member of numerous cycling teams during his career, perfect physique to fit on the bike, and probably one of the most talented athletes I ever trained with in terms of how he handled high intensity efforts. On a physical effort test, he always ranked among the best. He could really ham on the bike like no one else. One day, the two of us went for a long ride in the mountains. I remember about 1.5 hours into the ride and in one of the longest climbs of the day, he made his first move attacking me with unnatural force. In a few seconds after that, he had opened a gap of about 60 meters. Slowly, yard by yard, I could make my way back to his wheel, but not without reaching my anaerobic and mental limit. A few minutes later, he made his second move, as brutal as the first one with the same results. Then, his third and fourth attack, accomplished the same results as his first two. Finally, about 3 or 4 kilometers from the top, I gave it all I had left. I decided to attack him at least once before he left me in the dust. To my surprise, I saw him drop farther and farther back. On the top, once we regrouped, he told me that I was unbeatable. I responded with, "At what? It is not me, it is your lack of mental strength." Isn't it ironic that the most physically talented athlete can't perform at his best because of mental weakness? He gave up easily when things were not going exactly his way.

On the other hand, I remember Daniel Borras. He was kind of a "stocky" guy, always a little bit overweight, and not a great physically talented athlete. His best "weapon", though, was his mind. He was mentally capable to hold "the pace" as long as was needed, never failing, he was always there. If you ever had the intention of dropping him in a ride, you needed to be sure you could hold the pace till the end, because sooner or later he was going to be back on your wheel. More than once it happened to me that I relaxed after 15' to 20' break away, and in few minutes struggled with having him back again on my wheel.

In both cases we are talking about talented athletes, even though we need to classify them in completely different groups.

3.1 DIFFERENT TALENTS

3.1.1 Physical talent type 1:

We all are born with certain physical characteristics, some of them will suit perfectly to the specific sport and some others won't. It could be any physical condition that gives us an obvious advantage over the others. For example, the guy who is 6 feet 6inches tall has an obvious physical advantage over someone who is 5feet 10 inches tall, if they both play basketball. A marathon runner with a muscle composition of 90% slow switch fibers has a physical advantage over the runner who has 50% fast and 50% slow switch fibers composition, etc. Based only on this type of talent, races would be always won by the athlete with the suitable physique specific for the sport. Fortunately, for us all, there are other aspects that are as important, or more important than the physical talent type 1 alone. Luck, talent type 2, and mental talent also contribute to advantage.

3.1.2 Physical talent type 2:

Many of us remember a triathlete from the '90 and early '00 and former Ironman World Cup Champion, Thomas Hellriegel. More than once, he mentioned the quantity of massive hours of hard work he was putting in weekly in order to win the Hawaii Ironman. He may not have the best physical talent 1 of all the triathletes, but he had the talent that allowed him to train as much as he needed to be the best, without getting sick, injured, or breaking down. And we will call it physical talent type 2. As a clear example, I will mention again my friend Dave Reartes. He was the kind of athlete that could train only 3 days a week and perform as well as the majority of the cyclists training 5 days a week. One of his problems, though, was that he was incapable to train consistently more than 4 or 5 days a week, without getting mental burnout or physically injured. On the other hand, myself and others could train every day of the week and never tear down or burnout. Therefore, the results were a better performance than Dave during races even though he was a stronger physical talent type 1 than we were.

3.1.3 Mental strength talent:

To describe this attribute in short, we can put it in the group of all athletes that have the ability to push themselves to their physical limit as long and as often as they need to.

Finally, it must be mentioned, that all of us have our own mix of the three type of talents above referenced in certain grades and quantities. Sometimes, they will be great enough to allow you to succeed as an elite athlete, and sometimes (in the majority of most of us) "just" at personal level.

Chapter 4: THE THREE FACTORS FOR SUCCESS

4.1 TRAINING

How many times have we been disappointed in a race after weeks and weeks of long, hard hours of training? Or, just the opposite, we wonder about what we did for the last few days or even weeks that brought us to such incredible shape. We may ask ourselves, was it what I ate? Training is the most difficult subject of any sport. Some of the questions we ask ourselves concern how we train. When to train? Where to train? Is it my training that determines how I race? Is the way I train going to make any difference? Definitely, YOU ARE WHAT YOU TRAIN, no more, no less. The question to answer, though, is to know what kind of training works for each athlete. How much quantity? How much speed workouts or drills should I do in a training week? What aspects of myself do I need to improve? How am I going to improve? This is not only the key, but also what makes training such a difficult subject.

4.2 COMMITMENT

In the last few years, I tried without success to compete at high levels again. Time after time, something got in my way. There was always something important that had to be done before my workouts, something that ended up making my workouts shorter and different. The funniest part of my story, is that those things went from aspects in my life as important as my daughter's birth to eventually, things as little and simple as watering the plants in my back yard (and you know there isn't any rush to water the backyard plants). The message is clear; I don't have the commitment I need to compete at the level I wish. I may have the talent. I may have the time. I definitely have the facilities and friends, but I don't possess that level of commitment anymore that is required to compete at high levels. Certain aspects of my life changed since my days of high-level competition. Whether they were wonderful or new situations, bad habits, the wanderings of a brilliant mind, they all competed for my attention and I felt intensive training was not as important as what ever else I may have wanted to do at the time.

4.3 ENVIRONMENT

San Diego has been, since the beginning of triathlon history, the "Mecca" of the triathletes. Why? One word, "environment". San Diego has EVERYTHING athletes need for training. Number One, starting with weather, San Diego is sunny and warm almost 365 days a year. Second, San Diego has facilities. There is a lap pool with a master swimming program running all day in each neighborhood. Third, the people: friendly and fit as far as the eye can see. Fourth, rides: bike teams and roads with bike length wherever you go. Top former triathlete, Jurgen Zack, told me once when we were training "this is the perfect place to train."

There are other aspects to consider when we talk about environment. Aspects like family, friends, job, money, or something as simple as equipment all play a role in training and success. All of them can have a positive or negative effect and all impact on our training therefore, on your race performance too.

Chapter 5: STRESS AND BALANCE ON YOUR TRAINING AND LIFE STYLE

We only have a certain capacity to take stress. This stress, however, can come in different ways, shapes, and forms. Again, there is only that much we can take. Every athlete is different, and every athlete reacts to different activities in different ways. For example, on Sunday morning a group of friends and I used to go for a 3 hour ride where we put "the hammer down" two out of those three hours. For me, that did not increase my level of mental stress. But for some riders, it definitely did. On those days, it was easy for me to control what I ate and drank (as we all know food could be considered pleasure and therefore can be used to pacify your levels of stress) and my overall mood swings. Conversely, when we used to go for 6 to 7 hour rides, my stress level increased dramatically even though the intensity of the ride was much lower. On those days, and sometimes even the following day, it was hard for me to be disciplined with what I ate, or to control my poor mood due to the exhaustion. The reason, I have deduced, is because there is only so much we can self discipline and discipline is a kind of stress. As I said before, there is only so much we can control.

Stress is also accumulative. Some activities over and over and over, week after week, can produce mental burnout. If, on top of that, you have to keep training because a race is coming up, that could result in daily mental stress. Another example of stress, is knowing the following day's workout, this could provoke early symptoms of stress, leading you to a poor night of sleep. That's why some coaches prefer not allow to their athletes to know the full week's training schedule, keeping secret the daily training workout until the last minute. This way, they save the athlete from the pre-anxiety state.

But, as we said, stress comes in different forms and shapes. Suppose you are a competitive Age Grouper and you have been training for a specific race for 2 or 3 months. All of a sudden, your boss asks you to work extra hours or to travel more often or more days the following week. The first reaction of the athlete might be; "I don't want to lose my fitness level. Therefore, I will fit my training schedule in, wherever I can, in my already busy day." This busy schedule will increase the athlete's stress levels considerably possibly resulting in a fast burnout or a poor recovery from the workouts. One thing is for sure, the burnout will come. It may be a matter of time, but it will come. The timing depends in the ability of the athlete to deal with stress. As we already said, family issues, financial problems, and emotional problems could increase the levels of your stress as well. Therefore, it is important to manage the stress as effectively as you can until you can get back to your routine.

There are aspects in life that can increase your level of stress. There are also situations that can relieve it too. For example, the fact that an athlete is dating a girl and finds that he is in love with her could give him, at least for a period of time, a boost of stamina. Just think for a second that you got a bonus in your salary, or an increase in your pay check, I guarantee that will bring your levels of stress some units down in your stress graphic scale. Imagine that the race director is a friend of yours and he is taking care of your accommodations, meals, transportation, and baggage. This will certainly bring your levels of stress down.

Next there is an explanation in a simple graphic of the above explained.

Athlete capacity to handle stress in units:

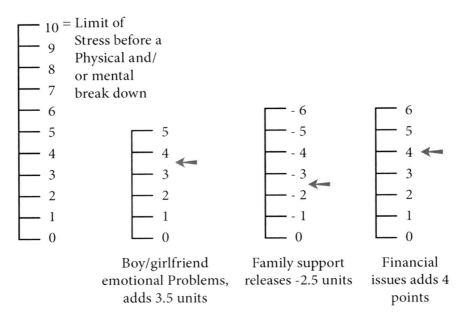

10 = Limit of
Stress before a
9 Physical and/
8 or mental
7 break down

Boy/girlfriend emotional Problems, adds 3.5 units

Family support releases -2.5 units

Financial issues adds 4 points

So, the total units of stress this athlete has are the result of adding the emotional stress of his/her relationship with his/her partner/wife/husband. That is about 3.5 units, plus his financial problems that are about 10 units, minus the family support that is helping him to relieve -2.5 units his stress. So the total of stress units this athlete is going to compete is a total of 5 units.

Note: The value of units will differ depending how important that factor is for the athlete. Example: family support may not be as important for you as it is for someone else. Therefore, the value of the units will be different, too.

5.1 PERFECT TIMING

When I was teenager, I used to race almost every weekend. In those years my percentage of podiums, not only as an Age Grouper, but also as an overall participant, was at a rate of 3 races for one podium. As I got older, the percentage was down to 10 to 1, then 20 to 1. Lately, my rate is even lower. In the last few years, I have been wondering what has change to make such a dramatic difference. At first, I thought maybe the quantity of training. But I know that at least half of the athletes that beat me, train even less than I do. Then I thought perhaps, genetically, athletes peak at different ages, meaning that some of them can reach their full potential at the age of 26, while others peak at age of 32 or even later. Greg Alexander won his second Hawaii World Cup Championship at the age of 37! Knowing that this could happen only in some cases, I also know that my ratio win/participation is too low for that to be the sole reason. Who doesn't remember a race where you pass an less fit boy or girl during the last mile of the race? I remember in 2005 I raced as an Age Grouper the Honu ½ Ironman. I was in a decent shape. I literally pushed myself to my physical and mental limit that day. Nevertheless, on the final miles during the run, a woman in her 40's and a younger man passed me. Adding insult to my personal frustration and ego, they were talking as if it were a Sunday morning walk on the beach. Why? How? What were the elements that contributed to my being overtaken by two somewhat, less fit individuals when, without conceit, I could definitely say I was in better physical shape?

For an athlete to achieve 100% possible score in a competition, several factors must be examined. Let's measure them in units. Then, let's list some (but not all) factors since everybody is different and there are thousands of possible factors that could affect an athlete's performance. Let's compare, at the same time, two athletes in two totally different situations. We will call athlete A Sally, and athlete B Edward. We will also give units from 0 to 10 to every factor in function of same race.

Athlete Sally.

Sally is genetically fit for the sport. She is a woman of 40 years old, about 130lbs, with 20% body fat. We will score this with 5points on this imaginary list.

Sally lives in the same town that the race is held = 10 points.

Sally is a mom. Her kids are college age and they and her entire family is at the race to cheer her on during the race = 10 points.

On race day, it is very hot. Sally, a local resident, is totally acclimated = 10 points.

Sally works in a part time, non-stress job from 9am to 1pm, Monday to Friday. She swims in the morning and has her second workout in the afternoon right after she finishes work. Everyday, her schedule is the same = 8 points.

She works out 15 hours a week, and 90% of the workouts are with her coach or social friends that help her with her workouts = 9 points.

She knows the people, streets, and roads of the race because she is local = 10 points.

She follows a clean and healthy diet, eats at regular hours and at relatively the same time each evening. She also cooks her meals at home = 8 points.

Her husband is taking care of all the logistics at the race = 10 points.

Her perception of mental energy is "good", her real mental energy level that day is good.

Athlete Edward

Edward is a 33 year old male of about 177lbs and 14%body fat, = 8 points.

Edward needs to travel from another state on a 5 hour flight = 4 points.

Edward comes by himself, and doesn't know anyone = 0 points.

Edward comes from much cooler state = 5 points.

Edward works all day, and fits his training (two workouts per day) in whenever he can. Normally, has to swim at 5:30am, and he needs to fit his second workout in during lunch time. Most days, he gets home after work at 9pm. = 5 points.

He always works out alone because every day his schedule is different = 4 points.

He doesn't know much about the race circuit because he just got there 2 days before the race = 4 points.

He eats whatever he can, whenever and wherever he can, usually fast food because it is what is most available on his trips and close to his job = 4 points.

The day of the race, he is rushing up and down all morning so he has everything set before the start= 5 points.

His perception of mental energy is poor, his real mental energy level on the race day is even worse.

In these cases, the man has probably a high mental fatigue from the accumulation of his daily life and race preparation, and possibly physical exhaustion.

Sally, on the other hand, is in a high and exciting mood, mentally and physically fresher.

Final score: Scoring from 0 to 100 being 100 the best possible scenario for an athlete performance. These are the results in this hypothetical Half IM race case.

Sally 75 points Edward 31 points

Sally	stamate race results based in the quantity of points	**Edward**	stamate race results based in the quantity of points
100 points	= 4:50 race time	100 points	= 4:20 race time
90	5:00	90	4h30'
80	5h10'	80	4h40'
70	5h20'	70	4h50'
60	5h30'	60	
50	5h50'	50	5h10'
40	6h	40	5h20'
30	6h10'	30	
20		20	
10		10	
0		0	

The results suggest that even though Edward is physically capable to race an estimate of 4h20' if all the factors in his life were perfect (meaning faster than athlete Sally), we realize that his physical talent can't match the disadvantage that he has versus Sally in other aspects of his life.

At some point of our lives, we all wonder how good of an athlete we could have been if the factors in our lives were the ideal ones, but this is why only few of us make it to the top. To illustrate, this may be why the Tour de France has only 160 riders, or why the IM World Cup Championship has only 100 pros out of 1700 participants.

Chapter 6: KNOWLEDGE AND EXPERIENCE IN THE SPORT

Often, I remember fond experiences related to my early participation in the sport. I think about how excited I was for everything, in part because everything was new for me. One of the things that still makes me smile sometimes, is to think about those days I was building my first triathlon bike, and how the bike shop owner used to sell me the most expensive equipment as if that was going to be the difference between winning or losing Sunday's race. How could I have believed that a titanium seat post (just to mention an example) 60grs lighter than the regular aluminum post was worthy of its $300 dollar price difference? And was that really going to make any difference in my race time? But the experience not only comes in that way, we also learn from our nutrition mistakes, or from our lucky "I didn't mean it but it totally worked, now I know" days, or simply, when the experience is telling you that you are over-training and that is time to back up. Again, knowledge and experience are part of the aspects that determines your peak performance level. Another example of that, would be those days when it is hard to know if you are really tired or just lazy. Usually, within the first hour on the bike, or the first 300 yards in a swimming session, you will know which one it is. Many times, over the course of my life, I experimented, as I like to say, with feelings of tiredness. In particular, I will always remember the time when former USA National Cycling Team member, Marci Mauro, and a pro-triathlete Marianne Ruetschi from Switzerland and myself were in a little village called Llansa, Girona, Spain for 5 weeks training and preparing for our next competition. One of the workouts was a 140 kilometer ride by the hilly coast of "Costa Brava" and a fast run afterward. That morning when I woke up, I felt incredible tired. I almost didn't even put my gear on. To be honest, for the first 30' on the bike I thought at least 10 times to turn around and ride back home. Finally, I had one of my best performances in those 5 weeks training camp on that day. On the other hand, I was training in Barcelona with my running partner, Pablo Amoros, ¼ into the run I had to turn around and walk back to the car, because I literally couldn't move my body any further.

Only experience teaches you to better understand your own body messages.

Chapter 7: BASE TRAINING; THE FOUNDATION

Base training is the foundation of your fitness. You don't race well only with it, but you can't adequately execute your specific training phase, or race phase without it. Your base training is going to help you to train properly. Your *speed work* phase, will help you at the same time to perform as wished on your race season.

Here are some orientation guidelines on how long it will take you to build the training base in order to get in to the final 10 weeks specific training phase before the race.

Ironman Triathlon Distance = 3 month or 14 weeks

½ Ironman Triathlon Distance = 2 month or 8 weeks

Olympic Triathlon Distance = 2 month or 8 weeks

Sprint Distance Triathlon = 6 or 7 weeks

Of course, if you have been in the sport for years even though the distance in time for the base training is the same, you will probably perform better every year on your specific training phase.

Chapter 8: HOW TO DETERMINE WHAT SPECIFIC TRAINING PROGRAM I SHOULD FOLLOW

In 1998, and while I was training for the Australia Ironman held in Foster-Tunkerry, I met a man who would later become a good friend and a good training adviser. His name is Domingo Catalan, former record man of the 100kms run (6h19'). I remember being in his sport running store called his same name in Barcelona, Spain. I mentioned to him that with my running partners, we used to run our long runs in between 3'50" and 4'15" per kilometer and my question was why always had to be so fast? The answer he gave me was short and clear. If you are planning to compete at 3'35" (6'8"/mile) pace per kilometer, to train at 4'10" (6'40"/mile) pace should feel easy. If it doesn't, it is because your expectations of how fast you can run on the race day are too high or unrealistic. Your goal should be slower times, so you can accomplish the times on your training days. On the other hand, don't expect to train slow and race fast, your body only will do what you train it for. So, in determining what training plan to choose, the answer is relatively easy. It wouldn't make sense to choose a program of how to train for the IM in about 10h, if the athlete can hardly average a speed of 18miles/hour on the bike in any training session or if he can't recover fast enough from the prior training session before it is time to put the hammer down again. In conclusion, choose the training program that you think objectively you can totally and not partially (swimming, biking or running) accomplish. Too high expectations only bring big deceptions.

8.1 WHY SPECIFIC TIMES, SPEED, AND DISTANCES

You are what you train. You will only be able to perform at your best at those races that have the format you train for. In other words, if you train short you will only be able to race well at short races. If you train at certain speeds, you probably will race into 10% of that speed. Therefore, you need to simulate in your training how you intend to race.

The body has an amazing ability to adapt and improve. It will learn what you teach it. However, the body will only learn the type of exercise for which it trains. A marathon runner does not necessarily need to be fast in a 100m sprint, even though he is training thousands of miles a year. Understandably, training needs to be as specific as possible. Another example highlighting this thought is Lance Armstrong. Although he won the Tour de France 7 times, he could only run a 2h 46' in his fastest marathon race.

8.2 LOAD

There is a well know theory called "body's compensation". When we stress our body or system physically, the body has an adaptation process reaction, leading, once is rested, to a better shape to absorb the load and/or stress in the following training session. It is for that reason that training loads may need to be greater and greater over time.

8.3 RECOVERY

Remember that after the training, our body is in worse condition than before we started the session. As we said in the "load" part, it is during recovering that body adaptation to the stress occurs. The greater is the recovering the greater is the adaptation.

8.4 TIME

Fitness level improvements don't occur every other day. Sometimes it seems that we haven't improved at all. Even worse, sometimes we go slower than in previous training sessions, but all of a sudden we most likely will feel an improvement spurt, and our times will drop significantly.

8.5 TRAINING LOAD INCREASES

Either the volume or intensity, or other aspect of the training needs to be increased gradually, or else the notion of "too much or too fast, too soon" will bring you straight to an over-trained state, or will make you peak too soon. When this happens, you will notice a decrease in your times and performances pushing you to a period of inactivity sooner or later.

Chapter 9: SHORT, INTERMEDIATE, AND LONG TERM GOALS

For a lot of athletes and mostly for triathletes, the year has one main goal. Usually, they concentrate on one race that is the most important. Perhaps an Ironman, perhaps the same triathlon he/she has competed in for years and has become a yearly tradition. For some of them, a smaller group exists a life career goal, which could be anything from taking part in the Olympics games, to qualifying for the Ironman World Triathlon Championship in Kona, Hawaii, as an Age Grouper, as an elite athlete, or just finish the triathlon itself.

In any case, the athlete needs to prepare and compete in races, usually shorter in distance prior to the main one.

These races far from putting pressure on the athlete are valuable to give her/him an idea of the level of fitness at that point, and the experience necessary to succeed in the major race goal of the year. Competition, then, is also the time to correct or even improve parts and aspects of your preparation, your racing tactics or your goal-setting strategy.

Chapter 10: BRAKING DOWN THE TRAINING BY COMPONENTS

10.1 TECHNIQUE

The definition of technique is a "systematic procedure or routine by which a task is accomplished". In a sport like triathlon that combines three different sports and two transitions in one event, technique and proper form is a fundamental factor. Part of the off-season should be dedicated to improving this aspect. It would be also well advised to put some attention on technique in our daily training regime. A proper technique will make you better athlete.

Why should I be good at technique? Why should I spend so much time trying the best technique? The answer is efficiency. Proper technique should be the most efficient way to move your body in a certain environment accomplishing the best result measured in distance, time, power, or energy consumption. Therefore, and specifically in triathlons, technique will help us go faster and/or longer with the minimum energy consumption.

10.2 DISTANCE AND DURATION

In some of the scheduled training days, you will see that it gives you certain distances by which to train. Some times are given in kilometers/ miles or meters/yards, other times are stated in minutes or hours. To understand the difference is crucial. The day's given in times, the goal for the athlete is to train the entire period, therefore the distance trained is not a relevant data. This avoids also, in huge measure, the over-training factor of not having to push yourself over specific distance when you are tired. And vice versa, when the workout is given in distance, the athlete needs to accomplish that exact distance, and the time to complete it isn't relevant. Sometimes, you will have tests where you will have to complete a precise distance in certain time. That will help you to know where you are in terms of fitness.

10.3 INTENSITY

Intensity is the effort required in any single training. This also can be given in the schedules by heart rate or personal perception. It is extremely important to strictly follow the intensity recommended in each workout. A long distance workout completed too fast will make you too tired to optimally execute your speed workout session. And again, a speed workout done way faster than indicated, could leave you too tired the rest of the week causing you to rest more, or cut short the rest of the week workouts.

10.4 REST PERIODS

Rest periods are those times where you take it easy (and you should really take it that way).

We have 3 types of rest periods.

1. The one in between intervals in the same training session. Those can come by time or heart rate.
2. The one in between workout sessions. They can go anywhere between hours to days.
3. The rest periods between seasons. Normally anywhere between, fifteen days up to a month.

In any case, they are as important as any of the training sessions.

Chapter 11: WEIGHT TRAINING

Lots is said about weight lifting and its benefits. There are; however, those who say just the opposite. But first let's look, in short, at the latest theories about weightlifting and its benefits for the athlete.

Let's analyze next formula:

> Performance = resistance of the muscle to the fatigue (measured in time or distance) + muscle strength input during that period of time.

That makes us think that in order to perform well in a race, we need not only to have good endurance, but also strength. Ways to develop strength:

1. Sport specific training; A cycling example would be intervals up hill with a long gear. A swimming example would be swimming with paddles, etc.
2. Weight lifting: Exercise duration, number of repetitions, as well as different muscles and exercises to choose, may be different for each sport.

Benefits:

- Improvement of the bone tissue density.
- Hypertrophy of the muscles: Improvement of the muscle fiber diameter due to greater protein synthesis.
- Increase in number and size of mitochondria.
- Improvement of the enzymatic activity = higher speed obtaining energy.

- Increase of ATP and CP reserves.
- Increase the storage of the glycogen in the muscle.
- Increase of the triglycerides up to 75%.
- Greater speed and quality of the nerves pulses as consequence of the development of the terminal nerves.
- REALLY IMPORTANT! strengthen of the tendons and ligaments (that could result in lower risk of injury)

Reading the points above, you might say that is totally necessary to incorporate weightlifting sessions or similar training into our training regime. And you may be right, but be careful.

11.1 WEIGHT LIFTING, YES BUT...

- Massive repetitions with low weight sessions are useless, unless you are rehabbing from an injury.
- Lifting too many times a week may make your muscles too heavy and big. Yes, you will have lots of power but you will need also a lot of oxygen to feed them.
- Never do weight lifting before an important training day because you may have soreness on the muscles you worked out.
- Never do weightlifting after a long running or biking training session. Your muscles microfibers are already exhausted, inflamed, and probably with micro tears due to the exercise. Lifting heavy weights could result from greater tears in the muscle to a serious injury. Beside that, your muscle can't lift as much weight as could being fresh, so what's the point then?

Carlos Civit and Norman Stadler after a training
session in San Diego, California

11.2 SPORT'S SPECIFIC TRAINING, YES BUT...

If we could incorporate power/strength training everyday into our
regime, that would be fantastic!! But the fact is that no body can recover
from that or handle that for a long period of time, not even for a short
period. Therefore, these are my recommendations:

- Don't do them before an important day (unless the session
  is really short in duration)
- Allow your body to recover in between day sessions. In
  other words, don't incorporate power/strength training for
  example Monday, Tuesday Wednesday of each week as they
  are too close to each other.
- Remember that a good, solid session could leave you dead
  legs for a few days.
- Don't confuse power/strength training with speed training.
  In the second case, you are more likely to be working inside

your anaerobic threshold, while in the first case, power/ strength, you only work inside your aerobic threshold.

11.3 WEIGHT TRAINING AND INJURIES

We are not born the same way. Some of us will have bigger quads, some of us will have stronger upper body, some of us will have a higher composition of slow switch fibers, some will have mostly fast switch ones. But one thing is for sure: all of us have imbalances in our bodies. You can take supplements for those imbalances that are in organs and blood. For muscle imbalances, there is nothing better than to work with weights. Through lifting weights, you can isolate a weak muscle, or teach it how to work in conjunction with other main muscles. You can also train your stabilizer muscles with some balance exercises with weight.

After so many years as a personal trainer and coach, it is really easy for me to analyze and detect muscles imbalances in my athletes. One, but not the only example, would be training a runner or a cyclist. Cyclists, in general, can lift much more weight in a leg extension exercise or squad exercise (involves mostly quads) than, in proportion, what they can lift with any hamstring curl exercise. Normally, the aforementioned is just the opposite for a runner. So again, lifting weights could be the right thing to do to even up those imbalances, perhaps even preventing future injuries. I must mention too, that the best time of the year for that would be the pre-season phase.

Chapter 12: THE PRINCIPLES OF TRAINING

There are basically three phases during your training season. First, the base or volume period, usually done in your pre-season or right before specific training season. Then, the specific training period, also known as speed training period. This one usually starts the last 4 to 12 weeks before a race. Last is the taper period which is always between last 21 to 4 days before the race, depending of how much you have been training the last 20 weeks and in what month of your training season you are at. (the farther in to the season you are the more miles you have in your legs, therefore the longer the taper needs to be).

12.1 DIFFERENT KINDS OF TRAINING AND THEIR TARGETS

1. Aerobic low-intensity training: this part of the training will build your fitness to be able to do the specific training phase. You can use this pace training on those times that you have an easy recovery day, a long and slow distance training session, or on those days that your main goal is to improve and work on only your skills and technique.
2. Speed workout:
2.1. Short and max or power sprints intervals:
    These kind of exercises won't help you directly on your race day, but they will definitely help to improve your overall times on your sub maximal effort intervals. Duration is anywhere between 30" to 1'.

2.2. Sub maximal effort intervals:
   This kind of workout won't help you directly on your race day
   either, but will help you to improve your overall times on your
   tempo/race paces or extensive intervals. Duration is anywhere
   between 1' to 4'.
   90% to 95% of your maximum effort exercises teach your body
   how to exercise with oxygen debt, and training you mentally
   to the stress of the pain of high-intensity efforts, and develop
   sub maximum pace.

2.3. Tempo/race pace maximum steady state or exhaustive
   intervals, 4' to 4h:
   This kind of workout will help you to perform your best
   on the race day, long time intervals, farleks, run tempo etc.
   Duration is anywhere between 4' to 4h. depending of the
   sport. This workout will also help you to get familiar with the
   intensity, and be able to manage the physical and mental stress
   of the race intensity or pace better. The tempo pace or a race
   pace should be the highest speed you can maintain for the
   entire length of the workout. Of course, it will depend of how
   fit you are at the time you train for it. My recommendation
   is that the distance of the workout can't ever be as long as the
   race you are training for. Up to 80% to 90% will be more than
   enough. Also it is important at this point, that we simulate
   race conditions, meaning profile of the race, temperature if
   it is possible (some athletes travel to more humid, and hotter
   states for their training), food and drink you will use also at
   the race day, and characteristics of the race in general. For
   example, if the race starts at 7am, you may want to have your
   first workout of the day consistently at 7am, so your body is
   used to being awake and ready to go at that time. Also, you
   may want to simulate the start of a race, sprinting the first
   300m before you get your tempo pace, I do it in my swimming
   workouts.

Finally, just to say that the length and duration of the intervals and
rest periods between sets need to be adjusted over time in the same
program. The intervals should be short with a long period of rest at
the beginning of the program and gradually increasing the duration of
them at the same time we decries the rest period, as we get closer and

closer to the race or as we are getting fitter. So for me, on my training, I used to start with short intervals of 200m to get fast and build up to up to 3000 to 5000m. I remember one of my most brutal workouts I used to do on Sundays where I did long rides up to 112 miles and right after intervals on the track that was next to my house. During the first weeks the intervals were 200m with long rests, my goal was just to get used to the feeling and stress of running fast right after the bike. One time, I went from 400's to 800's to 1000m, 3000m, 5000m up to 21k at race pace. Remember that not more than one race simulation can be done in a week. It depends on the athlete. Your body may only handle one every 2, 3 or 4 weeks. Most important, they should never be done 2 or 3 weeks (depending of the distance) before a race.

Specific training phase

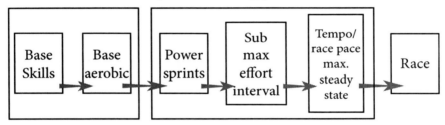

Chapter 13: OVER TRAINING

Over-training is the result of overloading your body with too much training; it could be too many speed workouts, or the right amount but at too high intensity, or too long and boring workouts, or too many races, or just the combination of all of them together. Call it excessive training at high-intensity or too many hours of it, all of it leads the athlete to a loss of performance and therefore a poor race results.

Over-training could come after many years of too much training or just after few seasons. It could decrease your performance 90% or 1% depending how deep in to the athlete is. In any case, it is always better to arrive at the race start 1% untrained than 1% over-trained.

13.1 OVER-TRAINING: A HARD WAY TO LEARN BUT NECESSARY

Envision a motorbike racer that needs to bring and incline his motorbike to its limit. He has to know the real limits of his motorbike before this breaks or he just falls in a curve. Just like this racer, a serious athlete will have to bring his body to its maximum capacity limit to absorb physical stress in order to perform his best possible. As with the motorbike racer, he eventually will fall in an over-trained state at some point in his career. As we mentioned in other chapters too, we over-train much faster and with lower load of training if our lives are complicated and stressful, compared to simple.

13.2 MAIN CAUSES OF OVER-TRAINING

There are hundreds of causes that can cause over-training. As we mention in previous chapters "stress" is a major one, but if we talk only in exercise terms these are the most common:

1. Poor recovering in between and/or races
2. Too much high intensity training, commonly known as speed training
3. Load increases , distances or duration of the workouts way over the capacity of the athlete to absorbe it
4. Too much competition
5. Too short off-season
6. Low variety of different workouts
7. Successive failure to achieve goals and lower performance at races than expected
8. Too many lonely workouts

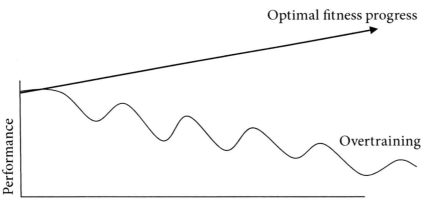

Time (measured in weeks, or month or years)

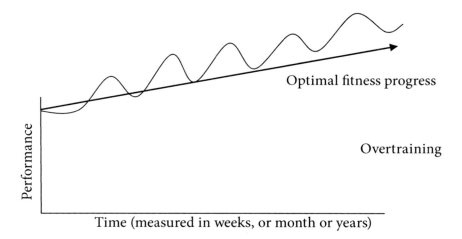

Over-training athletes may be doing less training than their peers, but due to such outside factors as medical problems or even their personal tolerance to physical activity, may fatigue more often and earlier. Remember, you only can train to the equal degree from which your body can recover.

13.3 WHEN DO I KNOW I AM OVER-TRAINED?

Every athlete experiences the symptoms of over training in different ways, with different symptoms, or even similar symptoms but in different order, time, and intensity. Actually it is very difficult sometimes for those who don't have a coach and train themselves to realize that they are over- trained. Some of the most common realizations are:

1. Excessive fatigue when training or resting
2. Loss of competitive drive at racing or training
3. Loss of drive on hard training sessions
4. Low desire to train, and long periods of rest between intervals or before starting the training session
5. Loss in interest in sex
6. Increase in anxiety, specifically before a workout
7. Increase of irritability and anger
8. Sleep problems, waking often during the night, waking up in the morning and not feeling rested

9. Too tired to concentrate in any activity
10. Always feeling too tired to do anything
11. Weight loss or weight gain
12. "Burning" feeling in your muscles
13. Too high body temperature
14. Irregularities in blood pressure
15. Inability to maintain training pace and distance
16. Menstrual irregularities
17. Craving in large measures, sweets and other pleasures, that may be a source of calm to you.
18. Constant thoughts about quitting training indefinitely

Over-training usually comes on gradually, but normally it hits you all of a sudden. That is why it is so hard for some athletes to realize and accept that it is time to cut it down.

Transition area

13.4 HOW TO PREVENT OVER-TRAINING

The best way? Get a coach. The coach not only will have more experience and knowledge about how to train to achieve the best results, but most important, has an objective point of view about how much and how hard you are training. They will give you a total impartial opinion about what you should do.

If you can't afford or don't have the opportunity of having a coach, the best rule of the thumb an athlete can follow is to rest all the days you wake up and you feel that you can't finish a workout. This means that if you are not already over-trained you are at the door of it. Lots of times during my career both as an Elite and Age Grouper, during the recovering weeks after a big race, I would realize how hard and how far I pushed my body during the training, how little I was resting (thinking I had enough), and how little I was sleeping compared to the intensity and duration of my training. There is no doubt that my self-motivation was taking me over my own limit and therefore over-training me. In more than one occasion, I was blind to the signs of over-training, fearing to miss workouts, and lag of fitness improvement when I was resting. All in all, it doesn't mean I didn't have good results competing; but I probably could have done the same or even more with less training and more rest.

Chapter 14: BREAKING DOWN THE SEASSON BY PHASES

14.1 OFF- SEASSON

I used to take 5 to 6 weeks completely off at the end of my race season. I couldn't even think about swimming or biking or running. I guess everyone has his/her own timing and duration for their rest period. Mine has never been less than 5 weeks, and some times up to two months, depending how intense or how long that season has been. A lot of my fellow athletes take much shorter rest periods, down to two weeks, and some of them take no rest at all for the entire year, competing the entire year in another sport. Personally I don't know how they do it; my body and my mind just need the rest if I want to start the new season even stronger. I always knew when I was ready. I would go from a total burn out state at the end of the competition season to a state of feeling enthusiastic about training again, then I knew I was ready.

In terms of dieting, I would say exactly the same. During the off season, I used to eat absolutely everything I wanted without being worried if I was putting weight on or not. Normally, yes, I used to start the new season with some extra pounds. To be honest, this never worried me much. I knew that in few weeks of base training I was going to be back to a training weight.

Carlos Civit

14.2 BASE OR VOLUME TRAINING

There is no doubt that in order to race well, we need to bring our training as close as possible (in terms of speed and pace) to our ideal race performance. At the same time to be able to get that close during our training we need to put some hours of "mellow" training in our body with three main objectives:

1. Increase our muscle efficiency to specific biomechanical movement
2. Increase our overall aerobic capacity and efficiency
3. Increase our cardiovascular, neuromuscular and arterial capacity

As we said in Chapter 10, these 3 aspects will give you the endurance you need to cope with the tempo and speed work that comes later in the program. It will also help you achieve your final pace on the race day.

I usually ask the athletes I train to divide the base training in two parts.

14.2.1 Phase I:

In this period, the athlete trains those aspects that will help him or her to become better triathletes. It's all about technique and drills. For example, if you think your swimming could be faster, improve your technique in the water. Yes, this IS the right time to train it. Leave the watch in the locker room. It is the time to train without the pressure of how much you swim or how fast you go.

On the bike portion, in this period, I always ask my athletes to train on a mountain bike and have as much fun as possible. They not only will build a good base, but also will increase dramatically their ability to control the bike in a sport where I have seen the most quantity of cyclist with the worst skills.

Triathlon is a sport in which you always move forward. So is running. Eventually over the years we create imbalances between the main muscles that we need when we generate the movement and those that aren't as important. These specific biomechanical movements usually work more like stabilizers. They create a lag of biomechanics efficiency that may eventually lead to injuries. In Phase I of the base training, I usually ask my athletes to incorporate plyometrics and weight training routines as a main workout in addition to running. This way we "smooth" the differences between "main" muscles and "secondary" ones.

14.2.2 Phase II:

The second phase of base training is, by far, the hardest for me; not only in terms of time consumption, but also in the mental aspect. I always say that here is where you can determine the serious athlete versus the recreational one. The serious athlete is the one that will do whatever it takes to get that best of himself vs. the one that practices the sport just for the fun of doing it. In Phase II the training is intended to improve your muscle efficiency as well as increase the aerobic capacity, the cardiovascular and neuromuscular, and arterial capacity.

During this phase, I am more worried about over-training my athletes mentally than injuring them through over-training them physically. As anecdotal evidence, I always mention my base training in 1997. I thought I was in my peak fitness level, and I had really ambitious goals.

Therefore, my specific training phase had to go accordingly to those goals which meant my base training had to be great in miles, distance, and total number of weeks. I trained 95% of the time by myself, always long and slow. Even though my body was adapting to the distance, and muscle fatigue was occuring later and later in the training, it wasn't the case with my mind. Each day I was more and more mentally stressed to the point that one day I woke up, and I couldn't even look at my bike. It is not because I was tired; I wasn't. It was because I was mentally over-trained. It took me 5 days without getting even close to my bike before I started to feel the desire to ride again.

In Phase II, mileage should be gradually increased. Training is still done mainly at low intensity but the volume of miles or hours will depend on the experience of the athlete, how many years he or she has been in the sport, as well as the goals and time available for it. Some days, these long and slow workouts are boring with a capital "B." It is for that reason that I always recommend to my athletes to train in groups in this phase. Speed isn't as important as duration. It's also important to remember that training too fast will only make you peak too soon and may even lead to injury. Finally, it must be mentioned that base alone does not improve performance greatly, but it is essential to your speed phase training which does help you for your race performance.

14.3 SPECIFIC TRAINING PERIOD OR PHASE

Once you have arrived at this stage, it is the time to start training as close as possible to race conditions. This means in terms of speed and pace, distances or duration, and race profiled. This specific training period is the critical time. You need to be physically and psychologically prepared to put the "hammer down". The following weeks of training is where most of your performance gains are made, where you will take full advantage of the tremendous endurance you have built up in the "base phase". It is time to train new aspects of your biological capabilities:

- Accelerations
- Power
- Top speed
- Tempo/race pace

Even though this phase is the most "fun" part of your year long training, it is also where most of the injuries and over-training pitfalls occur. Athletes easily forget that the more intensity you have in your workouts, the shorter the week's volume needs to be, and bigger the time to recover between workout sessions needs to be. On the other hand, it is not going to help you to train up to 30 hours a week if you can't achieve your theoretical training times and speeds. In other words, it will help you more if you rest one day in order to be able to do a 60kms bike ride at race pace the following day, than if you train volume the day before and then feel too tired and just ride the 60kms the following training session at sub-race pace.

It is important that when you choose any of the training programs that are in this book, you be realistic and honest about yourself. It won't help your training, the total amount of miles and speed workouts of any schedule, if the times and speed aren't as directed. In other terms, is unlikely you run an Ironman in 10 hours even if you follow the schedule to the "T" in terms of distance and duration, if you are not capable to maintain the speeds or achieve the times indicated in the majority of the workouts.

Also when you prepare a specific training plan you need to know how fast you need or want to go in any of the disciplines, and what kind of profile you need to compete on. It is not the same to race the flat ½ IM Florida (really flat profile race), as it is to race the hilly Monaco ones, or the brutal profile of the Wildflower ½ IM distance. So, try to train as close as possible to race characteristics, and try to choose the races that best fit your characteristics. In other words, don't go to Florida if you are a talented climber, or if you really are looking to put the hammer down on the bike.

14.3.1 TAPERING AND THE ART OF TAPERING

This is, by far, the most difficult time for the triathlete. The race is coming up and anxiety is increasing at the same pace as our doubts and fears. It is hard to stop training because there is something that tries to make us believe we are going to lose all our fitness; even worse, we are scared we are going to do something that will make us slow and maybe even fat! On these days, it is really common for Age-Grouper athletes to try something new (don't ask me why) such as a different diet, that in the end, only upsets the stomach. Some athletes even change their seat post on the bike, or the handle bar, or even the wheels. We all look for that last minute trick that is going to make a difference between a great race and a failed race. To be honest, I still haven't heard any trick that makes that happen.

What is the truth? Well, I think it is just the opposite from change. A vital element of getting ready to race is freshening up. Exactly when and how much you need to start reducing volume is determined by how long you have until the race, how long you have been training, and also at what point in your race season you are. It is not the same taper length for the first IM in the season, in which normally 2 weeks is plenty, as opposed to your last IM, which I always recommend 3 weeks. For Olympic distance 10 to 7 days should be enough and for sprint distance 4 to 7 days is recommended.

It is also worth mentioning that tapering is a real personal part of the training and what works for you may not work for someone else. This is what experience brings you. As another anecdote, I always mention the tales of one of the Spanish national champions who used to lift weights the day before a competition, which obviously worked for him, but definitely doesn't work for the majority of us. Some people prefer to completely take off the day before the race. Personally, I would rather train 30' to 45' really easy. Either way, tapering always involves reduction of training volume. Mark Allen, one of the most successful triathletes of all time said once, "I may not be the most talented athlete at the start field of the Ironman, but I certainly am the most rested."

Chapter 15: HEART AND HEART RATE MONITORS

In many ways, our hearts work like any other muscle. It contracts and it extends like any other it can be fit and grow in size. In this regard, we can say that heart efficiency is based on the frequency that the heart beats per minute and the quantity of blood it pumps.

Heart rate efficiency = frequency X volume of blood pumped

If the heart is unfit, it needs to beat harder to maintain the same blood volume pumped. Therefore, the heart of out-of-shape athletes will have to beat harder to supply the same quantity of oxygen to the muscles. Don't forget that the slower the heart beats, the more time it has to fill its ventricles with blood, and that means a stronger contraction due to the bigger stretch of the ventricle, which causes a bigger explosion of blood to the muscles to be supplied. It has been proven that the highest efficiency of the heart goes anywhere between your resting H.R, and up to about 160bpm where the heart starts losing its capacity to fully fill its ventricle or doesn't have enough time to fill before the next beat.

15.1 HEART RATE

As you know, the heart rate (H.R) is the number of times your heart beats per minute. This could be measured during exercise or during a rest period. The measurement can give us important data about the intensity of the workout, or our overall well-being if we measured heart rate during our rest time.

The number of beats per minute that our heart beats is most likely different from person to person. Depending on when the measurement is taken, it can vary depending on the intensity and duration of the workout, as well as other factors like heat, body dehydration levels, stress state, and overall level of body fatigue.

Even though it is a very important tool in our daily workouts, we shouldn't totally rely on it. Our H.R thresholds vary according to our fitness level. An athlete could run an all out effort 10km distance at the beginning of the season averaging 160 beats per minute. The same athlete, at the end of the season, could run it in much shorter time at a much lower average H.R. Additionally, the same athlete running the same distance at the same H.R but at his/her peak shape, could go not only faster but also be way below his/her actual anaerobic threshold. Translating this into our training sessions, suggests that every 2 or 3 weeks we should find our new thresholds, adjusting all the training to our new threshold limits. This could be accomplished by different methods. The most well *known*, however, are by testing our lactic acid in blood after a workout or measuring our H.R after a 100% max effort. Other factors that influence our heart rate, are how rested or tired you wake up that morning, how hot or cold the weather is, or even how dehydrated we may be. Finally, the duration of the workout and therefore the fatigue of the muscles directly affect our H.R.

I always mention to the athletes I train or coach, that one of my favorite workouts when I am in peak shape is to ride from the city of Barcelona to the village of Llansa (Costa Brava). From the last traffic light in Barcelona to the first traffic light of Llansa, it is exactly 160kms (100miles). One of my goals on those workouts is a solo effort maintaining exactly the same average speed over the entire ride, even though the second half of the ride is quite hilly. As the kilometers are going by, and mostly by the last quarter of the ride at the same effort, perception, and speed, my heart rate is always 20 to 30 bpm higher than the first quarter, depending how much muscle fatigue I am accumulating in my legs, how dehydrated I am, how hot or cold it is. Therefore, as we said, it is not always possible to follow the H.R monitor to the "T", even though there are some training sessions in the schedules that train with it as an imperative.

15.2 HEART RATES AND ITS NOMENCLATURE:

There is a lot written about the heart and its zones, but I am going to summarize the most important facts that I think an athlete needs to know.

1. H.R Max: That is the maximum times a heart can beat in a minute. This may be different for every single athlete, you can't train to improve it, and with age gets slower.
2. Resting H.R: Is the amount of times that the heart needs to beat when we are totally rested or resting. This can be improved in two ways: losing weight and becoming more fit. It varies in function due to our physical condition that day. If we are tired it will go slower, if we are over-trained it will go much faster, etc.
3. Lactic threshold: When the heart can't supply enough oxygen to the muscles, these keep contracting with an oxygen debt. The result of this is a sub-product of the muscle called lactic acid. This sub- product in great quantities suffocates the muscle getting to the point that it can't contract or extend anymore until the levels of the lactic acid turn down to lower levels or, until the intensity of the exercise decreases.
4. VO2 Max: This is the maximum volume of oxygen that we can use per each unit of time. That means it is our capacity to transport the oxygen from our lungs to the blood when we inhale a full breath. In other words, how much of the oxygen from our lungs can actually arrive or be transported to the blood, with the rest of it released with the rest of the nitric carbonic when we exhale.

15.3 H.R ZONES AND WHEN TO TRAIN THEM

After many years of training I have come to the conclusion that there are five ways to divide your H.R zones.

1. Moderate Active Recovering Zone: I ask my athletes to train in this zone during and right after the cool down or the day before a race. I also encourage this zone when they don't feel good due to the start of a flu, or any other sign of sickness.

They also should be at this zone when they are recovering from an over-training phase, recovering time in between intervals, and when they are recovering from an injury.

2. Aerobic Zone: This zone, for me, is mainly where an athlete can sustain a pace for long periods of time, mostly used during base training phase.

3. Anaerobic Threshold: High intensity workouts fit perfectly in this zone. We use it on our long intervals or really fast tempo workouts. It "hurts" and needs to be done few times in each training micro-cycle.

4. Red Zone or Full Anaerobic Zone: Short intervals in shape of long sprints, with lots of rest.

5. Power Zone: Short sprints at 100% of your full potential.

Example of workouts in different zones:

> Moderate Active recovering zone < 60% of your max H.R 30min. easy run or bike or swim

> Aerobic zone < 80% of your max H.R 3000m swim or 2h. ride or 1h. run.

> Anaerobic threshold zone < 90% of your max H.R 5 x 400m. swim or 3k run interval or 3x 10min. ride at race pace.

> Red or full anaerobic zone < 95% of your max H.R 10 x 100m swim or ride 10 x ½ mile hill repeats or 10 x 400m run

> Moderate Active recovering zone < 100% of your max H.R weight training up to 15 repetitions per exercise or 25m swim sprints or sprints up to 20seconds on the bike or 10 jumps up a high step.

Carlos Civit at the ITU World Championship

15.4 HOW DO I KNOW MY H.R IN EACH ZONE?

It is really difficult to determinate when you are in one zone or another solely based on your heart rate. There are too many factors that affect your H.R and determine your different zones. For example, as we said before, a really hot day can make your H.R raise 5 or 6 beats more per minute at the same exercise intensity than if it were cold. To be more or less hydrated also affects the quantity of beats. Are you over-trained or too tired? That means that your heart will beat slower, probably between 10 to 20 beats slower with the same intensity of exercise, etc. On the other hand, your fitness level switches every 2 to 3 weeks. This will not only make the different H.R zones move up and down, but will also change the amplitude of them.

Let's explain a graphic example. In October 1996, I raced after my off-season just for fun, it was a 9kms running race. Even though it was an all-out effort, I couldn't go over 160bpm if I wanted to finish the race. In other words, my aerobic threshold was up to 160bpm, anything above that was totally anaerobic. That same season, but 6 months later, I could run a full marathon on an average H.R of 175bpm. This is 15 beats per minute higher than my 9k run. On those years my max H.R was 197bpm in the first race and my aerobic H.R was anywhere between 140 and 160bpm. This was only 60 to 70% of my max H.R which gave me an amplitude of only 20 beats. In the second case, I was much fitter and my aerobic threshold was anywhere between 140 and 175bpm. This was between 60 and 95% of my H.R Max and with an amplitude of 35 beats, it left my anaerobic threshold with a much smaller amplitude.

Conclusion: Unless you have a lactic acid test or you do a max H.R effort test every 2 to 3 weeks, your work zones won't be completely exact, which pushes us to work simultaneously with our H.R monitor and our own perception of our effort. But not everything is so complicated. In all those years using H.R monitor, I found in it the perfect training partner. It helped me to control myself and not to go too fast on those days I was feeling way too good and excited and also helped me not to be too lazy on those intervals on track. Most importantly, it gave me day after day a referral of what I could do and what I couldn't in my workouts or races.

Finally we could use the Karvonen formula to find approximately our H.R zones:

$$\text{(H.R max − H.R rest) X \% exercise intensity+ H.R rest}$$
$$\text{= Specific H.R beats}$$

For example, if I want to workout in my base zone (60% to 80%) this is how I would calculate it:

$$\text{(195bpm − 39bpm) X 60\% + 39bpm = 132bpm}$$

$$\text{(195bpm − 39bpm) X 80\% + 39bpm = 163bpm}$$

I am going to workout not slower than 132bpm, but not higher than 163bpm. The amplitude of this zone is, therefore, 31bpm.

But again, that is only an approximation. Don't forget the example of the 9k run I gave you before.

Here are some possible circumstances to have in mind to interpret your H.R when training:

1. When you go too fast your H.R will go over the desired H.R zone.
2. If you are too tired, you may reach your speed (most likely not) but possibly not your target H.R.
3. If it is really hot and you have been sweating a lot your H.R will go easily over the H.R target with the same perception of effort.
4. If you are tired, the effort perception intensity will be much greater in order to reach (if you reach it) your target H.R.
5. If you have what is known as "dead legs" your H.R will drop immediately once you stop exercising.
6. If you are well rested your H.R will go easily over the target zone even within a comfortable effort perception.

Chapter 16: RECOVERING IS TRAINING TOO

More Recovery = More and Better Training = Better Race Performance.

This formula needs to stick in your head. The greater your recovery, not only in duration, but also in quality, the better your training will be and, in turn, the better your race performance will be. Your training is limited by two factors, how much physically you can do, and how fast and well you recover from it.

In my peak years in the sport I was so obsessed about recovering that I even bought a book about sleep and how to get deeper and longer in your REM zone. I knew by then, that was the key if I wanted keep training at the level I wanted.

16.1 SLEEP

Different people need different amounts of sleep, but one thing is sure: the higher is the activity during the day, the longer the sleep period needs to be. To be honest, I never met an elite athlete that slept less than 8 hours a night on a regular basis. In fact, the ideal for any serious triathlete is 9 hours per night.

The week previous to the race is important to maintain a good average amount of sleep with the night before the race being the exception. It is hard to find anyone at the Ironman start that had a great night of sleep. Things like nerves and sleeping in a different bed make it difficult.

What about sleeping pills? Even though I honestly believe that self-relaxation exercises produce better results, I admit that I took sleeping pills on multiple occasions to be able to sleep during the night. I did this not only before a hard workout day, or race day, but also on those nights that I couldn't sleep because I was too exhausted to do so. Do sleeping pills affect your performance the day after? It would depends how many pills you took the night, what kind of pills you took, and how long it's been since you took them at the start of your workout. Personally, beside the 30' of queasiness you may feel right after you wake up, I never noticed any difference in my performance, although I have read that studies have shown that you may underperform the following day. A good tip is not to try anything for the first time the night before your goal race.

It is important to realize also, the older you get the more difficult is to have a deep and long night of sleep. Most of the people I train over 40, rarely have 8 hours sleep. For those athletes, waking up during the night is common.

16.2 ENVIRONMENT

To be rested physically, you need to be able to rest mentally and emotionally. Without one, the other doesn't happen. I remember training in 1997 with Ferran, a great mountain biker. Together we did the most spectacular off road rides on the "Collserola" mountains in Barcelona, Spain. That year I had a few external factors coming together. First, I had to start an additional 4 hours of social service with work. On top of that, I moved to a new apartment where I had problems with a really noisy neighbor. I found that I couldn't sleep well 5 out of 7 nights a week. On the other hand, Ferran had the perfect lifestyle to be an athlete. He was married, with a 100% supportive wife, with an easy job living in a comfortable house. So even though I was training as much as Ferran, the difference between him and I was growing, not only mentally but also physically, week after week. Finally, I understood that not only was my sleep short, but it also wasn't deep enough. This led to a higher level of stress which was affecting my rest and recovery times, and contributed to a poorer overall fitness level.

For more on this topic, read "Stress and balance on your training and life style" chapter 5.

16.3 FLUIDS

Any hard training comes with an excess fluid loss which will slow you down, not only your recovery, but also during your next day's workout. Therefore, being aware of your drink intake is essential. A mix in quantity between water and sport drinks seems to be more than enough to hydrate yourself. I heard that some coaches sometimes ask to their athletes to train with no water, so they get use to the race conditions. That is the craziest thing I have ever heard about training methods.

16.4 NUTRITION

The healthier you eat, the better your performance will be over time. This doesn't mean that if you eat junk food one day you are going to lose all your fitness, but it will definitely affect you if you do it often.

16.5 MASSAGE - THE MAGIC TOUCH

Massage, after sleep, is the best way to recover and look after your body. Not only will your muscles recover much faster between workouts, but you will also prevent injuries. Massages stretch the length of the muscles and remove waste products which are a result of the workouts. They also increase blood flow to the muscles. A massage will free you from most of the knots and scar tissue built up in your muscles and tendons, and afterwards gives you an important feeling of relaxation. There are several massage types and techniques, as well as reasons to get them, but let's focus on sport massages.

Its main goal:

1. Prepare the athlete for the training session or race

2. Help with the recovery of the athlete
3. As a prevention of injuries
4. Treat and heal injuries

In all these cases, the technique of each massage needs to be different from one another.

Effect of the massage on the athlete:

- There is a great psychological effect on the athlete. First and foremost, it lowers the athlete's emotional stress.
- It also activates the blood flow, which eliminates toxins much faster and it even brings more nutrients that improve the recovery of the muscles and organs cells.
- Finally, there is the benefit of the massage dissolving muscles knots and ties.

When is the right moment for a massage? My experience tells me that a good, deep tissue massage can't be done right after a long and hard workout and never later than 3 days before your main race. Your day off is the best time to get one. One massage per week is highly recommended for serious and elite athletes, and 2 per month for a recreational competitor.

Chapter 17: INJURIES

We all have been injured at some point in our careers, some more than others. Biomechanical dysfunctions and strength imbalances have a lot to do with it. Injuries do not always mean we have to stop training. Lots of injuries like tendonitis, muscle injuries, bone stress fractures, or even ligament problems can only be noticed in a specific way and in a specific biomechanical moment. Sometimes, a running injury can't be felt on the bike or swimming. A shoulder problem that keeps you out of the water doesn't mean that you can't be on the bike for a cardiovascular workout. You can apply this to any part of your training, whether it's running, swimming, or cycling. For example, if you are training for a marathon and you have a foot stress fracture, you may want to suspend training for the run, but you may want be on your bike to maintain your cardiovascular capacity intact, so by the time you can re-start your specific running training, you are in decent shape. Lots of elite runners train on the bike on their off days, in order to maintain their endurance and to give their muscles rest from the pounding of running.

17.1 AGE, INJURIES AND LENGTH OF RECOVERING

Unfortunately, aging doesn't help. Who doesn't remember being a teenager when we all recovered from an injury with 2 or 3 days rest? Recently, a friend and I were joking about how slow the recovery process has become over the years. It got to the point where he named all his different injuries. He told me that at his age and from the time he reached 40, the injuries didn't go away that easily anymore. It can take months, even a full couple of years, to get to a level that isn't painful anymore. I have to say though, and to alleviate the fear of some of the athletes that could be reading this book, that appropriate medical consultation and injury treatment like proper physiotherapy, chiropractic work, massage, or even a properly planned training program, can and should improve the speed of the recovery. Eventually, this will totally heal an injury related to physical training.

Chapter 18: FLUIDS AND FOOD

18.1 NUTRITION

There is a lot said about nutrition, and there will probably be a lot more that will be said in the future as we see scientific advances and improvements in the field. However, I am going to mention what I think could be the most important aspect that an athlete should know without getting too much into the theme, because we could write a full book about theories and methods.

What ended up working best for me and I still follow it today if I don't train regularly, was a diet based on more carbohydrates in the morning and more protein in the evening. This culminated in a dinner based around salads, vegetables and protein. There is no doubt that if you eat well, your energy levels are way higher than eating a poor diet. The older you get the more you feel the difference.

Visual representations of the ideal food intake composition:

Day Activity: Day energy needs:

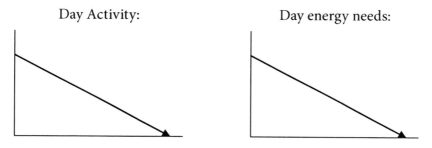

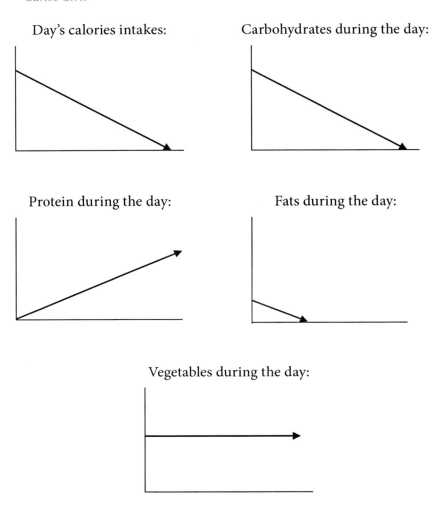

Day's calories intakes:

Carbohydrates during the day:

Protein during the day:

Fats during the day:

Vegetables during the day:

18.2 HOW MUCH AND WHAT TO EAT DURING TRAINING

There are different theories about how much the athlete needs to eat. You have probably heard or read that an athlete that trains 3hours a day, needs to have a daily caloric intake of about 3000kcal to 4.500kcal depending on his or her own body mass and weight. Are you the kind of person who is always trying to eat less to see if you can lose some weight?

Or are you the kind of person who eats all day and never gains a single pound? Normally, in general terms and talking about training methods, we could also catalog them in two groups with different names.

First of all, it is important to know what the perfect weight for an athlete is. Remember, an athlete in his perfect weight shouldn't gain or lose any weight during the week. I consider the perfect body weight to be that weight in which you perform your best in a specific sport. It is not the same to work to get a runner's type of body as it is to achieve the body type of an Olympic distance triathlete, even though in both cases they will probably have the same percentage of body fat. That is because their total body mass weight will be different. The runner doesn't need to have the upper body that a triathlete has, or even the big quads that a cyclist or triathlete has from cycling. In fact, in triathlons, and mostly if they are short distance, being skinnier doesn't mean necessarily faster. Power is a crucial factor in an athlete's performance, and that only comes with bigger muscle mass.

An example illustrating that can be seen in athletes like Christ Lieto, Jurgen Zack, or Spencer Smith. All of these great triathlete champions have big muscular bodies, but are also extremity lean. It is no coincidence that all of them were known for their phenomenal performance on the bike. That means that if your optimal body weight in which you have the best race results is around 175lbs, and let's suppose too that your are around 185lbs, even if you are lean and even if your body fat is only 8 -10%, your weight will still need to go down 10lbs if you want to perform as you desire. The only way to achieve that, unfortunately, is eating slightly less calories than what you burn during a full day. On the other hand, if you are one of those athletes that loses body weight daily unless you supply it with large quantities of calories, then most likely you will have to train just as much as you normally do and you will also need to eat more calories in order to maintain your optimal body weight.

Therefore, how much you need to eat will depend on 3 factors:

- What type of metabolism you have (fast or slow)
- What kind of athlete you are. Are you and sprint distance athlete or a marathon runner?
- How much body weight you need to gain or lose to get to your optimal performance weight? Do you need to put

weight on (probably muscle weight) or just get rid of those extra pounds?

18.2.1 MY PERSONAL EXPERIENCE

I read a lot about nutrition. The majority of the books say that the amount of calories you need to eat a day when you are training at full pace is between 3000 and 4500cal a day. However, my own experiences have told me that caloric intake is personal to each and every athlete and it also varies with age.

In my case, I perform much better when my intake of calories is lower as opposed to when it is way over. The perfect example is that when I was training for the IM New Zealand 2008, I also started to train for a marathon as part of the preparation for the IM at the beginning of the season. At that time, I was 185lbs. I began a diet of about 1500 to 2000cal a day of the healthiest food and most balanced diet possible. After a few weeks of poor performance and body adaptation, I went down 10lbs and my performance got better and better. After 10 weeks I was down to 163lbs and my training results were the best I had gotten in long time. I was faster than I was in years. Later on and after the marathon, I increased the hours of training and, of course, went back to a much higher calorie diet, up to 4000cal a day. The result was that I got bigger body mass, heavier weight, and my training performance, even though I was eating more, went down too. My conclusion was that after few months, a hypo-caloric diet didn't work for me and that my body didn't perform as well with diets over 3000cal a day no matter how much I trained.

Once, I read an article in a magazine about Peter Reid, 3 time Hawaii Ironman champion. One of the questions he answered was about how much he used to eat when he was training for Hawaii. His answer was, "I kept at home only the food I needed to eat that day. I was so hungry at bedtime that I had headache."

Finally, one more thing we need to account for is the fact that age is a big factor in your weight. As you age, your metabolism gets slower. It is more difficult to train harder more often, and the overall work volume decreases. This should affect your food intake. Growth hormones don't work as well when you are 50 years old than when you are 25, and that brings with it the fact that it is harder to get rid of the extra fat on our bodies.

I always say that in order to lose weight you need to burn more calories than you eat. Now, it is important to have the nutritional balance in those calories you take in. For example, you won't have the same energy and well-being with a diet based only in carbohydrates, than one that is based in a perfect balance between carbohydrates, protein, fat, vegetables and vitamins. Lastly, the difference in between in and out calories should never be greater than 500cal/day.

My final advice, though, is for you to find an expert in nutrition (sports nutritionist if it is possible) and design a diet that is the right one for you and your daily needs. Trust me, it really makes a huge difference!

18.3 WATER

Our body is 75% water. That makes us think that we need to maintain an intake of liquids during the day and mostly during and after training or competing. Studies have shown that a 2% water loss in our body could result in a 20% drop in our physical performance.

The perfect example of this can be seen in the retelling of my experience during the 2003 Camp Pendleton international triathlon. On that race, I lost my bottle of water during the bike length and while I still managed to get out of the bike third overall, on the run portion, the aids stations had only little plastic glasses of water, which was not enough to pacify my thirst. The result was that by mile 3 my legs couldn't keep the pace anymore, and having to walk, I ended up finishing in 12th position overall.

Having said that, I don't think we need to overdo water either. We all know that a large excess of fluid in our body could be as bad as not having it, and could even mean death, which is something that has sadly happened with competitors in the past.

Rule of the thumb: Don't wait until you are thirsty to drink. By then, it is probably too late and there is a good chance that you already have decreased your performance during the exercise. If you are racing, have a plan of where and how much you are going to drink and stick to it!

Personally, when I am very serious about a competition, or getting back to my highest fitness level possible, the first thing I do is stop drinking anything but water. This means no sodas, no beers, no juices, nothing but water and electrolyte products when I workout. I have seen that the results are quite significant. Just remember; you are what you intake.

18.4 CARBOHYDRATES

These are the body's "extra gasoline". Carbohydrates are one of the main types of food. Your liver breaks down carbohydrates into glucose (blood sugar). Your body uses this sugar for energy for your cells, tissues and organs. It is the fastest available source of energy for the muscles.

Carbohydrates can either be simple or complex, depending on how fast your body digests and absorbs the sugar. You get simple carbohydrates from fruits, milk products and table sugar. Complex carbohydrates include whole-grain breads and cereals, starchy vegetables and legumes. Complex carbohydrates and some simple carbohydrates provide vitamins, minerals, and fiber. This tells us that the intake of simple carbohydrates will be more beneficial during training and competing, and that complex carbohydrates will replenish our body once we are done with exercise.

Products made with refined sugar provide little nutrition. It is wise to limit these products after exercise.

18.5 THE FAMOUS LOW-CARBOHYDRATE DIETS

Carbohydrates raise blood sugar levels, which then kicks in insulin. The theory behind low-carb diets is that insulin drives blood sugar into the cells and prevents fat breakdown in the body. This means that you won't burn excess fat and lose weight. Now, if you're not eating the carbs, your body breaks down fat to provide needed energy. Some people do lose weight on low-carb diets, but the weight loss probably isn't related to the fact that they are breaking down fat in the state of sugar. Here are some of the reasons why I think you can lose some weight with low-carbohydrates diets.

1. When you initially decrease your carbohydrate intake, your body burns glycogen. Glycogen contains large amounts of water, so burning glycogen leads to the release of water and increased urination, causing weight loss.

2. You may have a decrease in appetite. Some of the clients I have been training over the years mentioned to me that they feel less hungry when they eat less carbohydrates during the day, so that leads to eating less, which ultimately ends in weight loss.

3. Most low-carb diets reduce your overall calorie intake because they strictly limit the variety of foods you can eat. Carbohydrates — including bread, pasta, rice, cereals, milk, most fruit and any sweets — usually provide over half a person's daily calories. On a low-carb diet; however, carbohydrates are limited or avoided, thus leading to a significant reduction in calorie intake.

18.6 PROTEIN

Protein is the juxtaposition of chemical elements called amino acids. One gram of protein is equal to 4 calories. Your body can use protein as a source of energy and actually will start doing it as soon as the body runs out of glucose. Recently, more and more athletes are switching to higher protein diets and some sport drinks are offering drinks with a higher protein percentage. The only "issue" is that it is generally agreed that low-carbohydrate diets tax the liver more in these processes than high-carbohydrate diets.

Again, my best advice is to eat healthy via a wide variety of aliments without thinking too much about the nutritional percentage of what you eat. Remember, no magical formulas or diets are out there that make you perform like a super human being. Poor diets, though, could destroy your fitness in a matter of weeks.

Protein is the "brick" of the body. It is the nutrient that the body needs in order to regenerate all those tears done to our bodies during a moderate activity or in intense levels of physical exercise. We can find protein in white or red meat, fish, eggs, milk, yogurts, cheese, full cereals, dry fruit, legumes, etc.

During my career, I tried all kinds of protein drinks, and amino acid supplements, mostly the complex ones. The truth is that when I had a healthy and balanced diet, I didn't feel any difference between taking them or not. In the case of the protein shakes, it should be noted that they are really high in calories and expensive. The real fact is that the body can only use that many grams of protein per "kilo" of body mass per day. In other words, it doesn't matter how much protein you eat, your body will only use what it can synthesize. The rest will stay in the blood for about 24h and later will be stored as body fat.

A classic example of misunderstanding the need of protein supplements is when you see guys who workout at the gym lifting weights for about one hour. They are more or less fit, but not lean. Right after the workout, they take a protein shake of 300calories or more thinking that will make them be bigger or perform better and recover faster. First of all, I don't think that 1 hour of a medium to high intensity weight lifting workout could damage your body to the extreme that a normal and balanced diet can't fix it. Second of all, you are asking for your liver and knees to work much harder when you abuse a high protein diet. Again, a normal and balanced diet should be enough to repair your body during the night.

In my personal experience, on those days I work out really hard or really long, a good red steak or white fish at dinnertime with a good salad is what worked best for me to recover.

In the past, endurance athletes have taken steps to maximize glycogen stored in the run-up to a competition by a procedure known as super-compensation. This involves the depletion of glycogen stores, followed by a period of carbohydrate loading, involving an extremely high-carbohydrate intake. My experience has provided me with no substantial change in your performance on race day. The fact that you are tapering the previous weeks before the race, allows your body to replenish your body glycogen storage with a regular diet, and may prevent your stomach from being upset due to the "last minute" diet changes. All in all, this super-compensation diet could bring about more inconveniences than benefits.

18.7 LIPIDS OR FAT

Fat is the body's greatest source of energy. Every gram of fat equals 9 calories! This is more than double a gram of carbohydrate, and is an almost endless source of energy. Imagine an athlete that weighs about 170lbs with a 10% body fat, which means that he is already very lean, with only 17lbs of body fat in his body. 1lbs = 250grms; 1grm of fat = 9cal. Therefore, he has 38.250 calories stored in his body that can be used to generate energy. Just to have a better appreciation, let's say that finishing an Ironman requires about 10,000 calories. That means that an athlete weighing 170lbs with 10% body fat has enough energy sources to finish almost 4 Ironmans. The problem is that it is not easy for your own body to use fat as a source of energy. The process of breaking down fat is really slow, almost too slow for sport activities, especially if they are high intensity. It should also be noted that certain organs in the body, such as the brain, work mostly with glucose.

18.8 MINERALS

Minerals are absolutely necessary in all of the body functions including muscle cells contraction and the neuromuscular tone maintenance. The most important minerals are calico, magnesium, iron, chloride, and potassium. We lose them in great quantities during training by our sudation. As a matter of fact, if you let your training clothes dry outside after an intense or long training session, you will see white marks of mineral salt all over them as the result of mineral loss with our sudation.

It is important to mention iron. Iron plays a part in the synthesis of the hemoglobin. Once, a sports medicine specialist told me that the simple pounding of our feet against the floor when we run may break down red cells, which are those who carry the oxygen to the muscle. I highly recommend taking iron supplements during long, hard and exhausting training periods, mostly if they involve running.

18.9 VITAMINS

Vitamins are indispensable. Normally we can obtain all of them in enough quantity in a healthy and balanced diet. An overdose though, could be fatal for the body, therefore "the more the better" philosophy doesn't work with the vitamins.

The main or most important vitamins for an athlete are vitamin C, all groups B, and vitamins A, D and E.

There are 3 ways where you can detect if you are taking too many vitamins. The first and most common sign is when your urine starts to be bright yellow. The second sign is that you may start having blisters inside your mouth. The last sign is that you will experience irritability and will have trouble falling asleep. Symptoms and side effects will disappear as soon as you stop taking the vitamins.

The need for vitamins increases with exercise, mostly for vitamin C, which eliminates the free radicals generated by exercise from the system. I recommend taking a higher dose of multi-vitamin supplements only for a short period of time when the athlete is feeling too tired even after resting, or when he/she is fighting any kind of common sickness.

18.10 NUTRITION ON RACE DAY

There is a lot published about nutrition on race day, and there are different things to consider:

1. Never try new things and "magic formulas" or new products on a race day. It is way better to race with those food and beverages that you have been training with.
2. It is a great help to have a specific and concrete plan of exactly how much and when you are going to eat and drink on the day of the race. Pro-triathlete, Marianne Rutschi, was

the master in following "the plan" during the race. Her first Ironman ever, 10h01'.

3. Practice in your long training days a simulation of that specific plan.

4. Remember that it is even possible to burn up to cal per hour in a race like the Ironman, but this doesn't mean we always have to intake that many calories per hour. Our bodies have already stored a huge quantity of calories in the form of sugar and fat during our typing training period.

5. Finally and most importantly, we can simulate race conditions on a training day very close, but it is never the same as that of the actual race day. Somehow on race day, it is much harder to eat and drink while we are competing. Our heart rate is usually higher on race day and we always are a bit anxious. The stomach usually has more problems at higher intensity to digest food due to the lag of blood in the digestive system at that point. Remember that the body sends the blood where it is most needed, in this case to our muscles. Therefore, it is not guaranteed that even if you have a plan and you carry the food and liquids with you during the race, you will end up taking them all or be able to digest them in a proper way. I always mention to the athletes I train that when I leave my bike in the transition area after the bike length in a race, there are still always energy bars stuck on the top of my bike frame.

Chapter 19: THOSE MIRACULOUS PRODUCTS TO ENHANCE FITNESS

Doping

Doping is considered the use of substances and methods designed to increase the athlete's performance in an artificial way with intentions of competing in an event. It could damage the ethics of the sport as well as the mind and physical integrity of the athlete. Having said that, it is difficult or impossible to find any product or supplement that can give us a substantial boost of energy or performance, unless it is considered illegal.

As a young athlete, I was always fascinated with all those products that appear every year in the market promising an incredible boost in performance. Since my early years in competition, I have read and researched every legal product in the market that could help in my recovery and overall fitness level. I went from the mythic L-Carnitine, to Quozime Q10, to electorococus senticousus, to the well-known product Siberian Ginseng. I even tried Red Bull and other energy drinks with tons of vitamins and caffeine, which ended up providing even more caffeine than our body should accept. But before we get into more details, I will say that I never found any 'legal' product that really enhanced my own fitness to a level that I could actually notice the difference in a short or moderate period of time. Here are my own experiences taking some of the products that are out in the market, products that I think work, and those that I feel didn't provide me any benefit at all when training or racing.

L-Carnitine:

L-Carnitine is a substance that theoretically helps your body to use body fat as a main energy supply. A perfect example is that migratory birds have a great amount of L-Carnitine in their blood, and again, only theoretically, it helps in delaying lactic acid from building in our muscles. It is said that 500 mg of L-Carnitine would be the perfect amount for an athlete. Now, in my own experience, I could not notice any difference at all when I was taking 500 mg or when I wasn't. I even tried it in a training session with my stomach empty and still did not feel any difference in my performance or energy levels.

Caffeine in energy drinks:

To fail a doping test you need to have the equivalent of at least 25 cups of coffee or 15mg of caffeine in your urine analysis. It is true that you can feel an increase in performance and well-being taking as little as one energy drink. The side effects that I felt; however, made me take these drinks out of my routine. First of all, it makes my body perform better on those days I am tired, which means I am only going to be more tired the following day. Sooner or later, I will have to take extra time off to recover. Second of all, I may perform better during a training day when I am fatigued, but it doesn't help me sleep at all. Therefore, I wake up even more tired. Third of all, it gives me palpitations and weird heartbeats when I drink them more often. On race days or those days in which I am totally rested, I don't notice or feel any benefit from drinking them. On top of that, my heart beats too high for too long during the performance. I have to say that on those days that I am really tired and I have an extra day off the following day, I may drink one energy drink before or during the workout.

Magnesium:

Magnesium is the 11th most abundant element by mass in the human body and is essential for good health. About 50% of the magnesium in our bodies is found in bone. The other half is found predominantly inside cells of body tissues and organs. A small percentage of magnesium is found in blood. Magnesium is needed for more than 300 biochemical reactions in the body. It is really important for athletes as it helps to maintain normal muscle and nerve function, keeps heart rhythm steady, supports a healthy immune system, and keeps bones strong. Magnesium also promotes normal blood pressure, helps regulate blood sugar levels, and is known to be involved in energy metabolism and protein synthesis.

There is an increased interest in the role of magnesium in preventing and managing disorders such as hypertension, cardiovascular disease, and diabetes. Magnesium is eliminated through the kidneys. In 1997 I read a nutrition book that stated how magnesium was fundamental in the contraction of the muscle, and also that taking a supplement pill of magnesium would make the muscle contraction more efficient. I took magnesium every day for a period of 3 months and never felt any different between training with or without, during, or after that period.

Rhodiola Rosea:

The perennial plant grows in areas up to 2300 meters elevation.

Rhodiola is known as a potent herb that helps the body adapt to stress in a healthy way. Rhodiola optimizes energy levels while promoting a healthy mood. Pilot studies on human subjects showed that it improves physical and mental performance and may reduce fatigue.

For 3 months I took a high dosage of Rhodiola while training for Ironman Germany. My maximum volume of weekly hours training was up to 30 and I added another 40+ hours of work per week to the schedule. I didn't feel any improvement in my mood, health, fatigue or overall wellbeing. Thus, I concluded Rhodiola was not having a remarkable effect on me.

Eleutherococcus senticosus (formerly Acanthopanax senticosus):

Siberian ginseng, also known as eleuthero, has been used for centuries in Eastern countries, including China and Russia. Siberian ginseng is a distinct plant with different active chemical components. It is prized for its ability to restore vigor, increase longevity, enhance overall health, and stimulate both a healthy appetite and a good memory. Recently, research has largely supported its use to maintain health and strengthen the system rather than using it to treat particular disorders. Siberian ginseng may help the body deal with physically and mentally stressful exposures, such as heat, cold, physical exhaustion, viruses, bacteria, chemicals, extreme working conditions, noise, and pollution. By strengthening the system, it may also help prevent illness.

The active ingredients in Siberian ginseng, called eleutherosides, are thought to increase stamina and stimulate the immune system.

During the 90's and for several years, I was taking a supplement of this root for months at a time and after every meal. During those years I got sick, stressed, tired, and never felt an increase in stamina of any kind. I didn't feel that my performance was better with it than without it and I'll go as so far to say that I never felt any different taking it. It has been years since I took it out of my daily supplements. I don't recommend it to any athlete that I train, and think there are better ways to spend your money.

GLUCOSAMINE:

Since glucosamine is a precursor for glycosaminoglycans, and glycosaminoglycans are a major component of joint cartilage, supplemental glucosamine may help prevent cartilage degeneration and treat arthritis. Studies reporting beneficial effects have generally used glucosamine sulfate. Two recent randomized, double-blind controlled trials have found no effect beyond placebo in reducing pain, while one found an effect beyond the placebo.

In 2007 I had knee pain related to a cartilage tear. I started taking Glucosamine supplements and after 3 weeks that pain was gone and has not returned since. I also have two testimonials from people who are physically active that had similar pain in their knees and shoulders and reported to me that after less than a month taking Glucosamine, the pain was gone. It would be hard to say if this was due to the Glucosamine or just the fact that the symptoms disappeared on their own, but for now I recommend to all clients that I train to try Glucosamine to treat any join pain before they contemplate any further treatment.

CREATINE:

Creatine was a really famous supplement in the 90's among athletes. It is certainly not a product that an endurance athlete should be thinking of. Known as "nature's muscle builder", professional and amateur athletes use it to increase their strength and performance. Creatine supplementation is claimed to increase muscle power by playing a role in the transfer of energy to help the muscle contract, which is important for short energy bursts such as sprinting and weightlifting, but useless in endurance sports. On top of that, supplementation may increase muscle body mass, which is what any endurance athlete is actually trying to avoid.This product is not recommended for any triathlete.

The "supplement world" is a market where millions of dollars are invested each year by companies that promise incredible results for those who take their products. Actually, if you read the label of any, and I mean any of these products, it seems that if you take them there will be an incredible difference in your performance. They write that you will miraculously go from a mediocre athlete to an elite athlete in a matter of days. They all promise you incredible results by explaining how their products work, and theoretically they may, but again this is only theory. Nearly 90% have never been proven to work, nor do they have studies extensive enough to prove their effectiveness. Remember, not everything is absorbed by our intestines or our digestive system, some supplements may work fantastically if they could be absorbed by our digestive system or stored somewhere in the body, but unfortunately the excess will always be eliminated by urine or excrement.

Now, to say definitively that none of the products I tried in all these years may have had a long-term beneficial effect in my body would be untrue. But, unfortunately, I won't live a second life to compare the differences.

19.1 HOW I TESTED THEM:

Some of the products like L-Carnitine, Creatine, etc. were tested in a workout. Sometimes I waited until I was really "bonking" before I took them to see if they had any real effect in my energy levels. I took some others like iron supplements, ginseng, and vitamins for long periods of time, up to a full season to evaluate the effects on me. I took some of them like vitamins or proteins right after hard workouts in order to evaluate the results.

As a personal reference, any other product I took during my career such as bee's pollen, royal jelly, and Rhodiola, which is also known as Golden root among others, never gave me the feeling of any substantial difference, either in the short or long term.

The recommendations for people that I train or those who ask me, is stop spending money with these products and invest it in a good sports nutritionist who will build a healthy and balanced weekly diet plan for you or will teach you good eating habits. That would be the best treat you can offer your body.

Chapter 20: THE LOG BOOK

Every single year I have been serious about competing, the first thing I did was either hire a coach or write my own training program. The second thing I always did, and still do, is to buy a training log book. It is amazing to see the differences between what we plan to do and what we finally end up doing. The log book will help you analyze the race results in a better way because it is recorded. In addition, it will help you to compare training seasons from one year to another. It will also give you a more realistic point of view of how you felt on prior training years. Sometimes what you remember and what truly was, is not always the same and the training logs help a great deal in this regard.

Chapter 21: HEAT

It can take up to 15 days to acclimate to hot, humid climates. I have also noticed that the fitter you are, the greater the adaptation is. A low percentage of body fat helps tremendously to acclimate better to the heat and improve your race performance.

There are lots of athletes that train in super hot places in order to get ready for their races, but how long and how effective is to be training in those conditions? There are two factors. One is, as we said, the better fitness level you have the better you perform in hot conditions, and the faster you adapt to the heat. The second factor is that it is also true that heat reduces your overall performance when training or racing. When I trained in Spain, I used to train harder and longer during the winter months, which are normally cool to cold temperatures, than on the summer months, which were hot and humid. Therefore, less training may equal a lower fitness level.

Chapter 22: MECHANICAL COMPONENTS

I am going to start this chapter by what I think is the evolution of the majority of triathlete's experiences throughout their careers. I will also use some humor by adding some lively sarcasm.

Let's divide the triathlete experience in 5 parts:

1. Total beginner and ingenuity.
2. Beginner
3. Experienced
4. 4. Elite
5. "Veteran"

22.1 TOTAL BEGINNER AND INGENUITY

I didn't know any better, so I didn't know that racing wheels could cut time off your bike splits. I also didn't know that a more comfortable outfit could make a difference. I now know that race shoes are for racing and that they are better and less used than training shoes. I have learned that carbon fiber makes bikes lighter and more comfortable. Lastly I didn't know about Aero helmets, or any other triathlon gadget out there, and still, in my first triathlon ever, with my girlfriend's borrowed bike, old dirty Nike running shoes and a sleeveless cotton shirt, I finished 8th overall. Could all those factors and "gadgets" really have made any difference?

22.2 BEGINNER

After my first triathlons I realized that participants were wearing different outfits and had "cooler" equipment that me, especially the top guys. So I started getting into the "better equipment better performance" philosophy. As soon as my budget allowed me, I bought my first triathlon bike, an $800 German 650cc wheel bike. I thought that having that bike was the best thing for me. It didn't last too long. It lasted until I trained for the first time with an amateur cycling team "Cyclist Club Gracia", they all laughed at how small my bike's wheels were. One of them told me "If they were so much better Miguel Indurain will use them in his time trials".

On those days I was aware of all technological advances for bikes on the market, last top try suits, or even goggles for swimming in the pool or open water. All of these products promised you great improvements on your P.R times, and all of them were really expensive too. I remember spending hundreds and hundreds of dollars in titanium and carbon fiber components, aerodynamic helmets, etc. What can I say, I had good races and bad races. Does it sound familiar? Does it sound, too, exactly like the supplement products? Yes, it does.

22.3 ELITE

Finally I got it! All in all, it is about your legs, self confidence, training and experience. There is no difference between $300 titanium seat post and a $25 aluminum one, no difference between your $200 try suit and your old-fashioned Speedo, no differences between your aerodynamic helmet and a conventional training helmet. (Just remember that Greg Alexander won his first Hawaii Ironman with the conventional bike helmet, in a year that almost all the other pros were wearing the aerodynamic ones). There are also no differences between carbon fiber handlebars and aluminum ones and there is no difference between a $3,000 wheels set or a decent pair of wheels set. It all comes down to your level of fitness, your level of self-confidence, your race plan, and your level of comfort with your gear. This is my humble personal opinion, though.

Some examples of what I mentioned above would be:

Tomas Helriegel: In his first ever Hawaii Ironman, he set the bike race-course record with a 36-spoke wheels set.

Miguel Indurain: Out of 5 Tour de France wins, he won his last time trial stage on his conventional road race bike, instead of riding his custom built time trial bike, called "la Espada".

Greg Alexander won his first Hawaii Ironman wearing his Newton race running shoes, but the running course record is still held by Mark Allen who won with his more conventional race Nike running shoes in 1995.

Dave Scott, in his first return to Hawaii after retirement, finished second overall at the age of 40 and his bike still had the shifter on the frame instead of on the tri-handle bar. He also ate Power Bars during the race, but Christ McCormack won his first Ironman title eating Clif bars.

So here is the ultimate question: How much are you willing to spend in your equipment /gear/products, and how much of that is just for how it looks? How much faster the makers say you will be versus how much faster you really become? Unfortunately, there isn't a clear answer and every individual athlete is different. Therefore, any answer will be correct.

Finally, I stopped getting intimidated by those super expensive bikes, wheels, wetsuits, secret drinks, or bars I saw at the transition area. I was finally able to look at my rivals as what they are: human just like me. I didn't have any excuses; it all came down to the days, months, and years of training and hard work.

22.4 EXPERIENCED

At the age of 40 I am back to my origins. I go to races sometimes with my old training shoes, or my training wheels. Nearly every time I drink a different electrolyte brand and eat different energy bar brands (normally the flavor I would like to eat during that race, I avoid trying new ones, though). What really makes a huge difference in my performance is my race plan, my tapering, how long I have been training for that specific race, and my expectations (which in all of the above, I got better over the years). One thing is for certain. I always get out there, the best of myself shining through, with no excuses.

Chapter 23: MOST COMMON QUESTIONS

Why is it the closer we get to the race the more speed training we should train and less quantity?

Our bodies have good endurance memory. Therefore, we can cut down the volume in the weeks prior to a race and we will still have the endurance. It doesn't happen the same way with speed and high intensity efforts. Consequently, I always recommend keeping some high intensity workouts until the same week of the race, although they need to be shorter and shorter in duration as race day approaches.

How much truth is behind the ideas of long and slow vs. intensity, as well as quality vs. quantity?

First of all, it is wrong to view quality as speed workout. In fact, a long and slow workout could also be an excellent quality workout. It just needs to be done when it is applicable. Having said that, my rule of the thumb is "Who trains slowly competes slowly". If you want break down your training in percentages I would say it is best to train with 75% of your time dedicated to a slow to moderate intensity and 25% focused in high intensity or speed training.

It is true that when you are swimming your H.R is about 10 bpm's slower than when you bike, and cycling is about 10 bpm's slower than when you run?

Yes, it is true. When you swim, your body is given buoyancy by the water and the main group of muscles being used is the arms. Arms are smaller than legs therefore they need less oxygen, which equals less blood that needs to be pumped. In cycling, we use the same muscles groups as we use in running, but our bodies are seated and that means a lower H.R. at the same intensity perception.

How much is too much when it comes to volume?

I have seen lots of athletes, specifically Age–Groupers that start doing their high-volume training really early and for way too long. Unfortunately, they get trapped in the philosophy of the more the better, which is quite common. At first, and since you are coming fresh from your off-season, you still have some speed in your legs. However, over time, that leads to an accumulative fatigue. By the time you move to the specific training phase, you are way too slow and tired.

Is it possible to have too much speed too early?

Some of us are really impulsive athletes. This occurs, for the most part, when you are young. Having little or no experience or patience with training moves, some athletes start doing intervals, or even races, with no fitness base build. With this kind of training philosophy, there is no doubt that in a matter of few weeks your body will start slowing down on those intervals. Worse, you may not finish the intervals or even finish your first race.

Why are warm ups and cool downs so important?

Warm up and cool downs are extremely important. Warm ups prepare the body for exercise. They are essentially designed to bring the temperature of our bodies higher. In this way, the blood starts going to those muscles that need it. If we are warming up while getting ready for a running race, the blood vessels in our legs are expanded to send more blood to legs and feet, leaving the other parts of the body with less supply. Also, there is a speed and strength enhancement. Furthermore, our body hormones like adrenaline glands start to work at higher levels and the physical chain of a carbohydrate and fat molecule start breaking down to supply energy to the body when it needs it. All in all, this allows your body to ready itself to handle bigger and greater efforts with less risk of injury and with more efficiency. This efficiency can be between 15' to 30' depending of the duration of the race should be enough, but remember that the older we get, the longer warm up we need.

Cool down: Exercise researchers say there is only one agreed-upon fact about the possible risk of suddenly stopping intense exercise without proper cool down. When you exercise hard, the blood vessels in your legs expand to send more blood to your legs and feet and your heart is pumping fast. If you suddenly stop, your heart slows down, your blood is pooled in your legs and feet, and you can feel dizzy and even pass out. There is also the theory that after an intense workout, the body generates waste products that accumulate and store in the muscles. This may translate to soreness in the body and affect the following workouts. Some recent studies, however, seem to prove that NOT cooling down has nothing to do with the next day's muscle soreness. An appropriate cool down should allow your body to return to its pre-exercise state and remove part of the residual products in your body improving recovery time. Of course, the cool down should progress in accordance with the intensity and duration of the workout or race.

That means doing any activity that gives your body a chance to gradually slow down the heart rate, reduce blood pressure and core temperature, and relax your breathing is recommended. Failing to ease out of any of these activities can lead to a sharp drop in blood pressure, which can cause light-headedness and, in extreme cases, a heart attack or stroke. 5' to 15' of moderate to easy exercise should be enough for the cool down phase. Stretching should also be part of the cool down as it assists in relaxing the compressed muscles preventing excess stress and injury to the body.

What about stretches? Should I do them? For how long?

90% of the athletes I know are in a tied schedule. Therefore, subconsciously we use the total time we have for training (swimming, biking or running), leaving the cool down and stretching for those days where we have more time. Guess what? Usually those days never come, or we use that extra time to fit in some extra miles.

Stretching is a good way to lengthen the body muscle and bring it to its original and most efficient work length size. Quick gains in range of motion help to improve an athlete's performance. A good range of motion creates better biomechanics, reduces fatigue, and helps prevent overuse injuries. Stretching will also improve the stiffness feeling we may have the first minutes when we wake up in the morning.

There are two kinds of stretches, the dynamic (not recommended at all) and the static. The static can be done in three ways. I recommend the PNF (proprioceptive neuromuscular facilitation). This consists of stretching the muscles for a few seconds and then contracting for few seconds in the opposite direction of the stretch.

In between 5 to 10 minutes after a training session should be more than enough time to have a good recovery and prevent loss of flexibility.

If I am traveling from another state or continent, how long before the race day should I arrive to the destination?

If you are traveling from the west to the east, it will take you much longer to acclimate that if you are traveling in the opposite direction. In general, I recommend 4 days per every 3 time zones that you cross. If you need also to acclimate to the temperature or altitude, no less than 7 days is recommended. Obviously, if you are an elite athlete that is going to compete in the Olympics or in a world cup championship a full month is suggested in any of the above cases.

When traveling long distances even if they are in the same time zone (for example from north to south America), I would recommend arriving no less than 3 days before the race day

Carbohydrates, why are they so bad for your weight and should I have a diet with no carbohydrates like some friends have recommend to me?

For every gram of carbohydrate stored in your body, 3 grams of water is stored, too. On the other hand, they are necessary for an efficient and ultimate performance. Also, after a meal really high in carbohydrates, you may feel sluggish. But if you can break through the first 20 minutes of exercise, you will be ready to maintain a high level of intensity for long periods of time.

Chapter 24: WHAT WE SHOULD CONTEMPLATE BEFORE WE START ANY PROGRAM

1. The majority of these programs are designed for specific athletes with their own needs, abilities, limitations, and background. These weekly schedules were built as the athlete was accomplishing them. The weekly athlete's report is a necessary tool in order to design the appropriate schedule for the following week of the program. The athlete's feelings, level of fatigue, and ratio of workouts achieved were among the indispensable data to create these programs. Consequently, these programs may not necessarily suit every one.

2. Go after realistic goals. The fact that you can follow one week of a specific schedule doesn't mean you can follow all weeks.

3. You may be really good atone sport, (let's say swimming) that specific sport's workouts may feel too easy for you, but you may have trouble following the schedule for the other two.

4. Don't follow the program if you feel you are getting over-trained. You may consider starting with a program for slower times more suitable to your fitness level at this point.

5. The times those athletes accomplished were the result of the equation:

    Years in the sport + talent + schedule+ race profile + age + race conditions (weather) = race finish time.

6. Races have all kinds of different landscapes and profiles. A hilly course makes the race slower than a flat course. Therefore, even if you follow to the "T" any of this book's schedules, you need to also consider what kind of profile your race has. For example: It doesn't take the same level of fitness to race Ironman Florida in hours as it does to race Ironman Lanzarote in hours. Lanzarote is much harder, and consequently much slower.

7. You may be doing just right with the training schedule that you choosed, but you may need an extra day off now and then. That is perfectly fine, take it!.

8. If for any reason you missed a workout, it is gone!, don't try to make it up in another day.

9. Some of the athletes of these programs are experienced, some of them have been in the sport for long period of time, therefore their bodies are quick adapting to the stress from the training.

10. All the training schedules have been designed and wroten by coach Carlos Civit. The athletes in this book have been chosen out of all the athletes he has trained for the past years. In some cases the names, some personal data, and race dates have been changed to protect the confidientality of these athletes.

TRAINING PROGRAMS:

Training for a sub 9 hours Ironman
Training for a 10 hours Ironman
Training for a 11 hours Ironman
Training for to just finish an Ironman

Training for a 4:15' to 4:45' hours ½ Ironman
Training for a 5 to 5:30' hours ½ Ironman
Training for just finish a ½ Ironman

Training for Sub 2 hours Olympic distance triathlon
Training for 2h30 hours Olympic distance triathlon
Training for just finish an Olympic distance triathlon

Training for Sub 1 hours Sprint distance triathlon

Training for Sub 1:30 hours Sprint distance triathlon
Training for just finish a Sprint distance triathlon

Schedules notes:

1. Training workouts in the left side of the outline square, means that the workout has been done in the morning. By other hand those in the right side of it, have been done in the afternoons.
2. Two workouts or more in one side, means they have been done one after the other, with a short period of rest up to 1h. in between them.
3. Brick: Two o more workouts done, one after another without resting time.
4. S.T: Means Specific training. You will see them in some of the schedules. Mostly reffering to bike workouts.
5. At the bottom of the schedules are notes wroten by the coach to the athletes to clerify some aspects of that week's training.
6. R: Rest time after an interval.

WEIGHT TRAINING ROUTINES
FOR THESE SCHEDULES

ROUTINE 1:		ROUTINE 2:	
Leg extension (quadriceps)	15 reps.	Cable cross over flys (pectoralis)	15 reps.
Incline Dumbbell press (pectoralis)	15 reps.	Close-grip lat pulldowns (back)	15 reps.
Sit-ups (abdominals)	25 reps.	One-dumbbell front raises (shoulder)	15 reps.
Seated low row (back)	15 reps.	Lunges with dumbbells (legs)	15 reps. each leg.
Seated leg curl (hamstrings)	15reps.	Crunches in 45 decline bench (abd.)	25 reps.
Shoulder dumbbell press (shoulder)	15 reps.	Low back extensions (low back)	15 reps.
Low back extension (low back)	15 reps.	Push ups (triceps)	15 reps.
Cable adductions (adductors)	15reps.	each leg Barbells curls (biceps)	15 reps.
Cable abductions (abductors)	15 reps.	each leg Machine adductions (adductors)	15 reps.
Preacher biceps curl with bar (biceps)	15reps.	Machine abductions (abductors)	15 reps.
Reverse push down (triceps)	15 reps.	Seated calf raises (calfs)	15 reps.
Standing calf raises (calf)	15 reps.		

ROUTINE 3:	
Close-grip Bench Press (Chest)	15reps.
Reverse Chin-Ups (Back)	15reps.
One-Arm Dumbbell Press (Shoulder)	15reps.
Concentration Curls (Biceps)	15reps.
One-Arm Reverse Pushdowns (Triceps)	15reps.
Gym Ladder Sit-Ups (Abdominals)	15reps.
Stiff-Legged Deadlifts (Low-back)	15reps.
Power Squats (Quadriceps)	15reps.
Cable Leg Curl (Hamstring)	15reps.
Seated Calf Raises (Calf)	15reps.

IRONMAN DISTANCE:

12 WEEKS TRAINING FOR A SUB 9 HOURS IRONMAN:

Athlete: Carlos Civit
Age: 27 – 28
Weight: 162,8 to 165lbs
Status: Single
Profesion: Pro. Triathlete, personal trainer and coach.
Base training prior to the program: 10 weeks averaging 20h a week
Time available for training: Schedule conditioned by work. Blocks of 3 to 4h training sessions, up to 6 hours a day
His best sport: Swimming
Groups: Majority of training alone. Running with a friend.

WEEK NUM. 1 FROM JANUARY 5 TO 11
1998 ((1Frst week of microcycle I):

MONDAY	
BIKING: (38miles = 2h30') Intervals up hill WarmUp + 3 x 20' up hill all out, resting on the down hill + Cool Down	RUNNING: 12.5 miles easy run (up to 153bpm) in 1h40'

TUESDAY	
BIKING: (40miles = 2h30') Nice and easy ride for 40miles	RUNNING: (track workout) W.u + 10 x 400m in 1'28" with 1'R Total = 4miles (50')

WEDNESDAY	
BIKING: (40miles = 2h30') Nice and easy 40miles ride on flats.	WEIGHT TRAINING + RUNNING: 1h.20' All body weight lifting + 45' easy running right after = 10km (6.2miles)

THURSDAY	
BIKING: (40miles = 2h) Nice and easy 40miles ride on flats.	RUNNING: (track workout) W.u + 3 x 1,500 in 5'20" 4'53" 5' with 2'30"R Total = 5.5miles (50')

FRIDAY	
BIKING: (49miles = 3h) 49 miles with 2 exercises of strenght training of 13km each	RUNNING: 12.5 miles easy run (up to 153bpm) in 1h40'

SATURDAY	
BIKING: (44miles = 2h45') 44 miles fast pace.	RUNNING: (51') 6.2miles at 6'48"mile + cool down

SUNDAY	
RUNNING: 18.75miles in 2h6' (between 6'20" and 6'48"/mile)	TOTAL TIME: 25h15' Bike: 245miles Run: 65miles Swimming: 0 Weights: 1 session

Notes from the athlete:
1.- Thursday intervals felt really hard, my legs were sore.
2.- Sunday: Run with my friend Pablo, he is running too fast for me, he is in a great shape.

WEEK NUM. 2 FROM JANUARY 12 TO 18
1998 (2nd. week of microcycle I)::

MONDAY	
BIKING: (47miles = 3h38') Hills	RUNNING (Afternoon): 7 miles easy run (up to 153bpm) in 1h10' with 12 x200m in 36" WEIGHT TRAINING(Evening): Full body weight lifting 1h.10'

TUESDAY	
BIKING: (34miles = 2h30') Intervals up hill WarmUp + 3 x 20' up hill all out, resting on the down hill + Cool Down	RUNNING: 12.5 miles easy run (up to 153bpm) in 1h41'

WEDNESDAY	

BIKING: (56miles = 3h40')
Nice and easy 56miles ride on flats and
  hills.
	RUNNING (Afternoon):
	8.75miles easy run (up to 153bpm) in
	1h16'
	
	WEIGHT TRAINING(Evening):
	Only legs weight lifting 1h.15'(only power
	  exercises)

THURSDAY	
BIKING: (37miles = 2h30') Nice and easy 37miles ride with specific bike workouts.	RUNNING: (track workout) W.u + 6 x 800m in 2'42" (2'R) Total = 10miles (1h.16')

FRIDAY
OFF

SATURDAY
BIKING: (63miles = 3h40') 63 miles easy pace on flats.

SUNDAY	
RUNNING: ½ Marathon "Granollers" = 1h17"	TOTAL TIME: 25h12' Bike: 240miles Run: 52miles Swimming: 0 Weights: 2 session

Notes from the athlete:
1.- Friday: I really feel overtrained intervals felt really hard, my
    legs were sore.
2.- Sunday: I felt perfect during the entire race. The start was
    really slow becouse there were too many People. Difficult
    profile.

WEEK NUM. 3 FROM JANUARY 19 TO 25
1998 (3rd.week of microcycle I)::

MONDAY	
BIKING: (30miles = 2h40') Hills	RUNNING (Afternoon): 6.2 miles in 49' SWIMMING (Afternoon): 1000m. In 22' easy WEIGHT TRAINING(Evening): Full body weight lifting 1h.15'(Less power more endurance training)
TUESDAY	
BIKING: (50miles = 3h30') All on the mountains.	RUNNING: 10 miles easy run (up to 153bpm) in 1h16'
WEDNESDAY	

BIKING: (35miles = 2h30')
Really nice and easy 35miles ride
   (133bpm Max.).
RUNNING: (track workout)
W.u + 2 x (1,500, 800m, 400m, 200m) in
   4'48", 2'40",1'16",32" with 2'30"R
Total = 8miles (1h15')
	WEIGHT TRAINING(Evening):
	Only legs weight lifting 1h.15'(only power
	   exercises)

THURSDAY	

BIKING: (37.5miles = 2h30')
Nice and easy 37miles ride with specific
   bike workouts.
	RUNNING:
	12.5 miles endurance run (up to 153bpm)
	   in 1h31'

FRIDAY	
BIKING: (50miles = 3h30') Really nice and easy 50miles ride (153bpm Max.).	RUNNING: 10 miles easy run (up to 153bpm) in 1h16'
SATURDAY	
BIKING: (62miles = 3h55') 62 miles on hills at tempo pace.	RUNNING: 15 miles easy run (up to 153bpm) with 2 x5K in 17' 17" in 17'46"
SUNDAY	
BIKING: (48miles = 3h) 48 miles on hills at tempo pace. RUNNING: 15 miles easy run (up to 153bpm) in 1h49"	TOTAL TIME: 33h36' Bike: 314miles Run: 77miles Swimming: 1000m Weights: 2 session

Notes from the athlete:
1.- Monday: Totally recovered from yesterday ½ marathon race.
2.- Sunday: It is sooo cold, I couldn't go for the 100miles ride planed
3.- I run everyday with Pablo, and he runs so fast!

WEEK NUM. 4 FROM JANUARY 26 TO 1 1998 (rest week):

MONDAY	
BIKING: (37miles = 2h30') Hills	RUNNING (Afternoon): 12.5 miles fast run (6'26"-6'38"/mile, up to 153bpm) Total 1h28'with w.u n 1h28' WEIGHT TRAINING (Evening): Full body weight lifting 1h.15'(Less power more endurance training)
TUESDAY	
BIKING (44miles = 3h): On the mountains. 18m/h average. SWIMMING (Afternoon): 1500m. In 30' easy	WEIGHT TRAINING(Evening): Full body weight lifting 1h.15'(Less power more endurance training)
WEDNESDAY	
OFF RAINNING!!!!	
THURSDAY	
BIKING: (36miles = 2h30') Tempo 36miles ride.	RUNNING: 12.5 miles endurance run (up to 153bpm) in 1h38'
FRIDAY	
OFF RAINNING!!!!	
SATURDAY	
BIKING: (50miles = 3h) 50 miles tempo, really windy, 22miles/h average.	RUNNING: 11.22 miles easy run (6'40"-6'50"/mile, up to 153bpm) Total 1h28'with w.u
SUNDAY	
RUNNING: 11.22 miles easy run (up to 153bpm) in 1h33'	TOTAL TIME: 13h30' Bike: 86miles Run: 48miles Swimming: 1500m Weights: 1 session

Notes from the athlete:
1.- Tuesday: Weather awful!! Feel tired I feel desmotivated
2.- Saturday: I felt super well on the bike!
3.- It has been rainning all week, difficult to ride the bike.

WEEK NUM. 5 FROM FEBRUARY 2 TO 8
1998 (1frst. Week of microcycle II):

MONDAY	
BIKING: (30miles = 2h40') Hills	RUNNING (Afternoon): 6.2 miles in 49'
	SWIMMING (Afternoon): 1000m. In 22' easy
	WEIGHT TRAINING(Evening): Full body weight lifting 1h.15'(Less power more endurance training)

TUESDAY	
BIKING: (50miles = 3h30') All on the mountains. RUNNING: (track workout) W.u + 4 x 1500m in 5'2", 5'3", 5'5", 5'13" (2'R) Total = 6miles (52')	SWIMMING (Afternoon): 1000m. In 25' easy

WEDNESDAY	
BIKING: (35miles = 2h30') Really nice and easy 35miles ride (133bpm Max.). RUNNING: 12.5 miles endurance run (up to 153bpm) in 1h28'	WEIGHT TRAINING(Evening): Only legs weight lifting 1h.15'(only power exercises)

THURSDAY	
BIKING: (50miles = 3h15') All on the mountains, 18m/h average.	RUNNING: (track workout) W.u + 6 x 800m in 2'44"/2'41"/2'37"/ 2'36"/2'35"/2'42" (2'R) Total = 6miles (1h.)

FRIDAY	
BIKING: (68miles = 3h40') 68 miles on hills at tempo pace hilly course. RUNNING: 11.25 miles easy run (up to 153bpm) in 1h33'	RUNNING: 12.5 miles endurance run (up to 153bpm) in 1h31'

SATURDAY
OFF

SUNDAY	
BIKING: (77miles = 4h20'total) 77 miles on hills at tempo pace. With city traffic I still average 23.75m/h. RUNNING: 11.25 miles easy run (up to 153bpm) in 1h32"	TOTAL TIME: 30h3' Bike: 315miles Run: 60miles Swimming: 1000m Weights: 2 session

Notes from the athlete:
1.- Monday:Felt really good on the bike.
2.- Thursday track workout: My legs were dead!
3.- Saturday I took it off becouse I had stomag flu.

Carlos Civit

WEEK NUM. 6 FROM FEBRUARY 9 TO 15
1998 (2nd week of microcycle II)::

MONDAY
BIKING: (36miles = 2h30')
On the mounitains.
WarmUp +
3 x 20' up hill all out, resting on the down hill + Cool Down

SWIMMING:
1500m. In 40' easy

RUNNING:
5.6 miles easy run (up to 153bpm) in 47'

TUESDAY
BIKING: (38miles = 2h30')
Nice and easy ride for 38miles

RUNNING:
12.5 miles endurance run (up to 153bpm) in 1h28'

SWIMMING:
2.400m. In 1h10' Moderate intensity intervals.

WEDNESDAY
BIKING: (56miles = 3h30')
Tempo pace 53miles ride only hills.

SWIMMING:
1.500m. In 40' Fast intervals lots of rest.

WEIGHT TRAINING:
1h.15' All body weight lifting

THURSDAY
BIKING: (53miles = 3h30)
Tempo pace 53miles ride only hills.
Average 18m/h with city traffic.

RUNNING:
12.5 miles endurance run (up to 153bpm) in 1h27'

SWIMMING:
2000m. In 50' Fast intervals lots of rest.

FRIDAY
RUNNING: (track workout)
W.u + 6 x 200m in 31" to 33" +
3x 1500m in 4'57", 4'50",4'58"
with 2'30"R
Total = 7.1miles (1h11')

SWIMMING:
1.750m. In 45' Fast intervals, lots of rest.

WEIGHT TRAINING:
1h.15' All body weight lifting (power exercises)

SATURDAY
RUNNING:
W.U 2 miles + ½ marathon in 1h.24'
(between 6'9" and 6'28"/mile)
Total time = 1h.39'

BIKING: (72.5miles = 4h)
72.5 miles all out pace. Really hilly.
Average. 19m/h with city traffic.

SUNDAY
BIKING: (73.5miles = 4h)
W.U 7miles + 59.3 race pace (22,5m/h average) + 7 miles C.D.

RUNNING:
16.8miles in 2h6'

TOTAL TIME: 34h49'
Bike: 328.3miles
Run: 69.6miles
Swimming: 7.575m.
Weights: 2 session

Notes from the athlete:
1.- Tuesday: I couldn't ride the 110miles planned becouse I flat 5 times!
2.- Friday run intervals with Pablo super hard!!!
3. Sunday : I wasn't pushing, not even feeling my legs and I averaged 22.5m/h!!!

WEEK NUM. 7 FROM FEBRUARY 16 TO 22
1998 (3rd week of microcycle II) :

MONDAY	
SWIMMING: 2000m. In 45' easy	RUNNING: 10 miles easy run (up to 153bpm) in 47'
TUESDAY	
OFF	
WEDNESDAY	
RUNNING: 12.5 miles endurance run (up to 153bpm) in 1h27' with 3 miles in 6.3, 6.8, 6.14miute/mile. SWIMMING: 1.500m. In 40' Fast intervals lots of rest.	WEIGHT TRAINING: 1h.15' All body weight lifting
THURSDAY	
OFF	
FRIDAY	
BIKING: (25miles = 1h40') 25 miles really easy	RUNNING: 8.75 miles W.U + 5k in 15'37" + C D . Totaltime: 59'
SATURDAY	
RUNNING: W.U 2 miles + ½ marathon in 1h.24' (between 6'9" and 6'28"/mile) Total time = 1h.39'	BIKING: (64.3miles = 3h45') 8.1 miles Easy run in 1h4'
SUNDAY	
RUNNING: ½ Marathon "Montornes" = 1h21' Really hilly course!!!	TOTAL TIME: 13h10' Bike: 89.3miles Run: 52.5miles Swimming: 3.500m. Weights: 0 session

Notes from the athlete:
1.- Tuesday: I was tired mentally and physically. Lots of anxiety
2.- Thursday: I need to take the day off. Too tired.

WEEK NUM. 8 FROM FEBRUARY 23 TO 1 1998 (Rest week):

MONDAY	
SWIMMING: 2500m. In 1h.10' easy	

TUESDAY	
BIKING: (36miles = 2h55') Nice and easy ride for 36miles all on mountains. RUNNING: (track workout) W.u + 10 x 400m in between 1'7"and 1'11" with 1'30"R Total = 6.8miles (1h10')	SWIMMING: 2.400m. In 1h10' Moderate intensity intervals.

WEDNESDAY	
BIKING: (30miles = 2h) Tempo ride for 30miles all on mountains.	SWIMMING: 2.500m. In 1h. Easy intervals. 100m at 1'30"pace.

THURSDAY	
BIKING: Interval up mountain: 13.25miles all out. Total time 54' RUNNING: 20 miles endurance run (up to 153bpm) in 2h16"(6'6"/m.aver)	SWIMMING: 2000m. In 50' Fast intervals lots of rest.

FRIDAY	
BIKING: (21.5miles = 1h30') Tempo ride for 21miles all on mountains.	RUNNING: 12.5 miles endurance run (up to 153bpm) in 1h28'

SATURDAY	
OFF	

SUNDAY	
OFF	TOTAL TIME: 14h3' Bike: 100,2miles Run: 39.9miles Swimming: 5.000m. Weights: 0 session

Notes from the athlete:
1.- I had to take this week really easy. Feeling really tired!
2.- Weather is so hot!!!
3.- Sunday race: Really hard, too many hills

WEEK NUM. 9 FROM MARCH 2 TO 8 1998
(1frst. week of microcycle III):

MONDAY	
BIKING: (62miles = 4h) On the mounitains, really easy.	RUNNING: 10 miles tempo run (up to 153bpm) in 1h12'
TUESDAY	
BIKING: (42,3miles = 3h) W.u + 12 x 1'20"interval up hill with 5'R+C.D	RUNNING: (track workout) W.u + 6 x 800m in 2'36" to 2'40" (slow!) with 1'R Total = 4.8miles (54')
WEDNESDAY	
BIKING: (36miles = 2h30') Really easy ride only hills.	SWIMMING: 3.000m. In 1h10' Fast intervals lots of rest.
THURSDAY	
BIKING: (72.5miles = 3h45') Tempo pace 72.5 miles ride only hills. SWIMMING: 3.300m. In 1h10' Fast intervals lots of rest.	RUNNING: 13.1 miles endurance run (up to 153bpm) in 1h34'
FRIDAY	
BIKING: (60miles = 3h30') Ride only hills.	RUNNING: 11.25 miles easy run (up to 140bpm) in 1h30'
SATURDAY	
SWIMMING: 2.000m. In 1h. Really easy	RUNNING: 12.5 miles tempo run (up to 140bpm) in 1h28'
SUNDAY	
BIKING: (95miles = 5h30') Really easy ride hills and flats. RUNNING: 5.7miles easy run in 47'	TOTAL TIME: 33h00' Bike: 367.8miles Run: 57.6miles Swimming: 8.300m. Weights: 0 session

Notes from the athlete:
1.- Felt flat and sick all week long

WEEK NUM. 10 FROM MARCH 9 TO 15
1998 (2nd week of microcycle III):

MONDAY	
SWIMMING: 3.000m. In 1h Fast intervals short rest, average for 100m 1'30"	RUNNING: 10 miles tempo run (up to 153bpm) in 1h16'

TUESDAY	
BIKING: (58miles = 3h45') 58 miles on mountanins. RUNNING: 10.6 miles nice and easy in 1h20'	SWIMMING: 2.400m. In 1h10' Long intervals short rest.

WEDNESDAY	
BIKING: (88miles = 5h) 88 miles time trial really hilly. RUNNING: 11.2 miles nice and easy in 1h32'	SWIMMING: 1.300m. In 35' Cooling down.

THURSDAY
OFF

FRIDAY	
BIKING: (60.5miles = 3h40') Easy ride (135bpm max)	RUNNING: 12.5 miles endurance run (up to 153bpm) in 1h33' SWIMMING: 2.900m. In 1h20' Fast intervals lots of rest.

SATURDAY	
BIKING: (70miles = 3h45') Really easy ride hills and flats. RUNNING: 12.5 miles easy run in 1h40'	RUNNING:

SUNDAY	
Duathlon Banyoles 6.2Run + 26.25miles Bike + 3.1Run 36'21" + 1h 13' + 19'20" = 2h9'40"	TOTAL TIME: 28h55' Bike: 304.37miles Run: 67.5miles Swimming: 9.500m. Weights: 0 session

Notes from the athlete:
1.- Saturday ride. Brutal ride with the cycling team Gracia. They destroyed my legs!!
2.- Brutal duathlon, good race test. My legs were tired from all week training but I still performed very well.
3.- Tuesday. Last run with Pablo, he race this weekend and is done for this seasson.

WEEK NUM. 11 FROM MARCH 16 TO 22
1998 (3rd week of microcycle III)::

MONDAY
SWIMMING: 3.650m. In 1h20' Long intervals lots of rest. (Part of the workout 4 x 500m in 8'04", 7'42",7'51",8'1")

TUESDAY	
BIKING: (70,8miles = 3h45') All mountains.	SWIMMING: 3.150m. In 1h30' Long intervals short rest

WEDNESDAY	
RUNNING: 12.5 miles nice and easy run (up to 140bpm) in 1h34'	SWIMMING: 2.500m. In 1h10' All out intervals up to 200m. lots of rest.

THURSDAY	
BIKING: (91miles = 4h47') W.u + Race pace + C.d	RUNNING: 10.6 miles endurance run (up to 153bpm) in 1h17'

FRIDAY
RUNNING (OFF day): 6.2 miles easy run (up to 140bpm) in 59'

SATURDAY	
SWIMMING: 4.000m. In 1h30'. Really easy Swim pace = 400m at 5'56" pace	RUNNING: 12.5 miles tempo run (up to 140bpm) in 1h38' Pace in between 6'16" and 6'40"

SUNDAY	
BIKING: (36.25miles = 2h) Really easy ride hills and flats. RUNNING: 18.75miles easy run in 2h25	TOTAL TIME: 23h Bike: 216.8miles Run: 41.8miles Swimming: 13.400m. Weights: 0 session

> Notes from the athlete:
> 1.- Felt terrible till Saturday.
> 2.- Saturday run in between
> 3. Sunday. New bike, just went out for a first tune up ☺ Couldn't sleep last night, wake up really tired.

WEEK NUM. 12 FROM MARCH 23 TO
29 1998 (1Frst week tapering):

MONDAY
SWIMMING: 3.000m. In 1h30' Long intervals.(Pace = under 1'30" per 100m)

TUESDAY	
RUNNING: 12.5 miles tempo run (up to 140bpm) in 1h29'	SWIMMING: 1.000m. In 30' Cool down

WEDNESDAY
OFF Trip to the Ironman

THURSDAY
OFF Trip to the Ironman

FRIDAY
OFF Brutal Jet lag

SATURDAY	
BIKING: (23.1miles = 1h30') Really easy ride hills and flats. RUNNING: 5.6 miles nice and easy run (up to 140bpm) in 40'	SWIMMING: 1.500m. 25'. Open water swim in the race lake.

SUNDAY	
(Same workout than yesterday) BIKING: (26.1miles = 1h44') Really easy ride hills and flats. RUNNING: 5.6 miles nice and easy run (up to 140bpm) in 40' SWIMMING: 1.500m. 25'. Open water swim in the race lake.	TOTAL TIME: 8h53' Bike: 36.8miles Run: 18.75miles Swimming: 7.000m. Weights: 0 session

Notes from the athlete:
1.- Brutal flight to Australia and brutal jet lag.
2.- Saturday. I feel sick, I think I got the flu in the plane.
3. Horrible road pavement

WEEK NUM. 13 FROM MARCH 30 TO
5 1998 (2nd. week tapering):

MONDAY	
(+ - Same workout than yesterday) BIKING: (31.8miles = 1h44') Really easy ride hills and flats. RUNNING: 5.6 miles tempo pace run (up to 140bpm) in 40'	SWIMMING: 2.000m. 30'. Open water swim in the race lake.

TUESDAY
OFF

WEDNESDAY	

BIKING: (13miles = 45')
Ride one loop out of the two loops
    marathon
	RUNNING:
	6.2 miles nice and easy run (up to
	    140bpm) in 42'
	Run one out of the 4 loop marathon run.

THURSDAY	

SWIMMING:
2.000m. 35'. Open water swim in the race
    lake.
	RUNNING:
	5.6 miles nice and easy run (up to
	    140bpm) in 40'

FRIDAY
BIKING: (28miles = 1h 20') Ride one loop out of the two loops marathon

SATURDAY
OFF

SUNDAY	
IRONMAN RACE!!	TOTAL TIME: 7h. Training + Race. Bike: 185miles Run: 43.75miles Swimming: 8.000m. Weights: 0 session

Notes from the athlete:
1.- Brutal heat! It is sooo hot!.
2.-Felt terrible all week, really heavy.

7 WEEKS TRAINING FOR A
10 HOURS IRONMAN:

Athlete: Marianne Rutschi (Female)
Age: 32
Weight: 130lbs
Status: Single
Profesion: Pro. Triathlete in Oylimpic distance since 2002
Base training prior to the program: 20 to 25h a week
Time available for training: Every day and hours
Her best sport: Swimming
Groups: With a partner. Swim masters at Boys and girls club
Goal for the seasson: Ironman Florida (her first Ironman distance) in
10h.15'

WEEK NUM. 1 FROM SEPTEMBER 28 TO 3 2.004:

MONDAY	
TUESDAY	
BIKE: 120km =4h Nice and easy (up to 75% of your max H.R)	TRACK: 1h. 20 x 200 in anywhere between 41" and 45" (100m walk in between) Coll down 10' easy jogg at 5'18"x km
WEDNESDAY	
RUNNING: 1h. 1h run at anywhere between 4'32" and 4'44"x km	SWIMMING: 4.000m Intensity: Up to 90% of your max HR
THURSDAY	

BIKE: 2h30'
Specific workout (1): 45' w.u + 4 x 5' as
    fast as possible (you need to ride at least
    over 40kms/h the entire time) + 5' rest
    Cool down
Intensity: up to 95%
	RUN: 16km
	16km at 4'32" to 4'44"pace

FRIDAY	
SWIMMING: 5.000m =1h30' Intensity: Easy (Up to 75% of max H.R)	OFF
SATURDAY	
BIKE + RUN: 160km + 35' 160km at 32,7km/h average right after 35' run at 4'28" to 4'37" Fast transitions.	
SUNDAY	
RUN: 21kms Run 21kms at 4'32" to 4'44" x km	TOTAL: UP TO 20h

NOTES:
1.- O.k this is your first week. So since I don't know you that well, don't be afreid if you can't make some of the workouts we will reatjust them in time.
2.- Tuesday: Go easy on the bike what is important is the run workout. There is no warm up on the run, just leave the bike on the track and start runing the intervals right away.
3.- Saturday: 32,7km/h is your race pace, so you will have to find a road where you don't have to stop that much and do your first time trial of 160kms on the bike at that pace. Short transition and run 35' right after.

WEEK NUM. 2 FROM OCTOBER 4 TO 10 2.004:

MONDAY	
OFF	

TUESDAY	

BIKE: 120km =4h
Nice and easy (up to 75% of your max
    H.R)
	TRACK: 1h.
	15 x 400 in anywhere between 1:32" to
	    1'36" (rest as long as you need to be
	    able to finish the intervals in the times)
	Coll down 10' easy jogg at 5'18"x km

WEDNESDAY
SWIMMING: 5.000m Intensity: Easy.

THURSDAY	

BIKE: 1h30'
Specific workout (2): Today's workout:
    ACCELERATIONS!!
(On a flat road) Useing only the longest/
    hardest gere you have you need to
    accelerate from 10 kms/hour up to
    45 kms/hour as fast as possible, then
    change gere and slow down for 4'.
    Repeat the exercise 6 times.
Cool Down_.
	RUN: 21km
	21km at 4'32" to 4'44"pace

FRIDAY	
SWIMMING: 5.000m =1h30' Intensity: Easy (Up to 75% of max H.R)	OFF

SATURDAY
BIKE + RUN: 160km + 35' 160km at 32,7km/h average right after 35' run at 4'28" to 4'37" Fast transitions.

SUNDAY	
RUN: 2h' Run at really low intensity.	TOTAL: UP TO 19h

NOTES:
1.- Track workout: Longer and faster! Right after the bike.
2.- Swimming just do the distance, don't push at any time.
3.- Bike workout, in the morning,short but intens,. Run on the afternoon after a nap.
4.- Saturday: I would like you do the same loop you did last Saturday. It will give you confidance.
5.- Sunday: your long run. Here you just want to work your muscular endurance and your bio-mechanics, so just take it easy and finish the run.

<u>WEEK NUM. 3 FROM OCTOBER 11 TO 17 2.004:</u>

MONDAY
OFF

TUESDAY
RUN: 45'   Run at really low intensity.   Nice and easy (up to 75% of your max H.R)

WEDNESDAY
FARTLEK RUN: Warm up 20'   10' (4'32") + 8'(4'55") + 8'(4'20") + 6'(4'55") + 6'(4'10") + 4'(4'55") + 4' (4'00") + 2'(4'55")   + 2' (3'50") + 1'(4'55") + 1'(3'40")   Cool down 10' easy jogg.

THURSDAY	
SWIMMING: 5.000m =1h30' Intensity: Easy (Up to 75% of max H.R)	BIKE: 1h15' Nice and easy ride. It is mostly to get ready for tomorrow.

FRIDAY
RUNNING + BIKING: 40' + 2h   40' Steady run 4'28" to 4'37" x mile   Right after, bike time trial (1)

SATURDAY
RUN: 2h'30"   Run at really low intensity

SUNDAY	
SWIM +BIKE + RUN: 5K +160km + 15' 5.000m at medium intensity + 160km at 32,7km/h average right after 35' run at 4'28" to 4'37" Fast transitions.	TOTAL: UP TO 16h50'

NOTES:
1.- All right!! We start the tapering = less hours of training and more specifics workouts.
2.- Friday: Your first specific workout on the bike, (you will have 2 more). We will do this one all together. Kathy, Marci, some other top group athletes and I.
3.- Sunday: Your last very long day. Do the swim like if that was the only thing to do that day.

WEEK NUM. 4 FROM OCTOBER 18 TO 24 2.004:

MONDAY	
OFF	
TUESDAY	
SWIMMING: 5.000m Intensity: Easy	
WEDNESDAY	
BIKE:2h Specific workout (3): Today's workout: TEMPO! (On a flat road) 5'at 40kms/h + 5' easy 4' at 42kms/h + 5' easy 2 X (all of them) 3' at 44kms/h + 5' easy 2' at 46kms/h + 5' easy 1' sprint + 10' easy Cool Down_..	RUN: 15km 15km at 4'32" to 4'44"pace
THURSDAY	
SWIMMING: 3.000m =1h10' Intensity: Easy (Up to 75% of max H.R)	
FRIDAY	
SWIM +BIKE + RUN: 4K +140km + 15' 4.000m at medium intensity + 140km at 32,7km/h average right after 15' run at 4'28" to 4'37" Fast transitions.	
SATURDAY	
SWIMMING: 2.000m =1h10' Intensity: Easy (Up to 75% of max H.R)	
SUNDAY	
RUN: 2h30' Run at really low intensity	TOTAL: UP TO 16h10'

NOTES:
1.- More tapering = less hours of training and more specifics workouts.
2.-Tuesday: I will call you to workout together.
3.- Sunday: Still your long run, but much shorter.

WEEK NUM. 5 FROM OCTOBER 25 TO 31 2.004:

MONDAY	
OFF	
TUESDAY	
SWIMMING: 5.000m Intensity: Easy	
WEDNESDAY	
BIKING + TRACK: 3:30'h. Nice and easy biking up to only 150bpm	TRACK WORKOUT: 3 x 2.000m in 8'37" TO 8'52" (rest as long as you need to repeat the interval at the same pace!!!)
THURSDAY	
OFF	
FRIDAY	
SWIMMING: 3.000m =1h10' Intensity: Easy (Up to 75% of max H.R)	
SATURDAY	
RUNNING + BIKING: 30' + 2h 30' 30' Steady run 4'32"to 4'44" Right after, Bike time trial (3)	
SUNDAY	
RUNNING: 1h15'Nice and easy run (up to 155bpm)	TOTAL TIME: 11:25 hours

NOTES:

1.- First tapering week. You just have two really hard workouts on Wednesday and Saturday, the rest of the week you should recover as much as possible. Now, those 2 workouts need to be done at your highest leve of intensity.

2.- Saturday: We will repeat exactly the same workout we did with Kathy, Dennis and Marci. The goal here is to get the hightest average speed possible. No excuses!. We will leave every 45" seconds apart.

3.- The track workout is going to be more specific, longer and harder, and needs to be right after the bike, so leave the bike on the track and without warm up start doing the intervals.

4.- From now on your goal will be rest and recover as much as possible in between days and workouts. That means : 9hours of sleep a day, lots of drinks, lots of healthy foot (prohibit any forme and quantity of junk food).

WEEK NUM. 6 FROM OCTOBER 25 TO 31 2.004:

MONDAY
OFF
TUESDAY
SWIMMING: 5.000m Intensity: Easy
WEDNESDAY

BIKING + TRACK: 3:30'h. Nice and easy biking up to only 150bpm	TRACK WORKOUT: 3 x 2.000m in 8'37" TO 8'52" (rest as long as you need to repeat the interval at the same pace!!!)

THURSDAY
OFF
FRIDAY
RUNNING + BIKING: 30' + 2h 30' 30' Steady run 4'32"to 4'44" Right after, Bike nice and easy.
SATURDAY
OFF
SUNDAY

RUNNING: 1h15'Nice and easy run (up to 155bpm)	TOTAL TIME: 11:25 hours

NOTES:
1.- Marianne, from now on is all about resting. There isn't anything in the next 2 weeks you can do to improve your fitness. The most important thing now is get your levels of stress as low as possible.

WEEK NUM. 7 FROM OCTOBER 1 TO 7 2.004:

MONDAY	
RUNNING: 10km nice and easy = 50'	SWIMMING: 2.000m. In the race swimming length. Easy = 40'
TUESDAY	
BIKING: 2h. Nice and easy biking 2 hours.	
WEDNESDAY	
OFF	
THURSDAY	
BIKING: 2h. 2h really easy to the bike length.	
FRIDAY	
RUNNING : Up to 10km really easy to the run length	
SATURDAY	
SWIMMING: 500m at the start line.	
SUNDAY	
IRONMAN FLORIDA Race time: 10h1' Overall place: 4th.	TOTAL TIME: 6h.30' + Race

NOTES:
1.- Marianne, rest, rest, rest. There isn't anything this week you can do to improve your fitness. The most important thing now is get your levels of stress as low as possible. Try to set up your mind for the race, and think about like it is one more workout.
2.- Good luck!!!

11 WEEKS TRAINING FOR A SUB 11 HOURS IRONMAN:

Athlete: Mark Barnett (Male)
Age: 48
Weight: 160lbs
Status: Married
Profesion: Owns his own company
Base training prior to the program: 16h. a week
Time available for training: 18 hours a week conditioned by work
His best sport: Good runner.
Groups: Runs with a group and group ride on Saturday.
Goal for the seasson: qualify for Ironman World Championship Hawaii.

WEEK NUM. 1 FROM MAY 9 TO 15 2.005
(1 frst. Week microcycle I):

MONDAY
OFF

TUESDAY
BIKING: 3h. 3h. medium pace up to 150bpm.

WEDNESDAY	
SWIMMING: 3.500m 3.500m = 75% free style + 25% other strokes Intensity: Easy.	WEIGHTS + RUNNING: Weights: You need to follow the exercises of the routine 1. Execute 15 repetitions per exercise and switcht to the next exercise, and repeat the routine 3 times. Really short rest between exercises. This time, once you finish the 3 times, run 45' at easy pace = 8'40" to 9'/ mile.

THURSDAY
BIKING: 3h Nice and easy biking. (135bpm max) with S.T 1: : W.U 10 x (3'standing up at 60rpm and at 90% tension on the bike + 1' as high cadence as possible with no tension + 5' regular pace and tension) Cool down till you ride the 3h.

FRIDAY	
SWIMMING: (no more than 1h 10'.) 3.500m Intensity: Easy.	RUNNING: 1h 1h easy run = 8'40" to 9'/ mile

SATURDAY
SATURDAY WORKOUT = 4hours + track 4h moderate biking + 3 x 1mile at 7'00" with 3' easy jogging in between + Cool down Intensity: Moderate to low on the bike, whatever it takes on the run.

SUNDAY	
SWIM : 5.000m. nice and easy swim.	TOTAL TIME: 16h55'

NOTES:
1.- First week of volume.
2.-Saturday is a key workout, don't miss it.
3.- Sunday will be your long swim day

WEEK NUM. 2 FROM MAY 16 TO 22
2.005 (2nd. Week microcycle I):

MONDAY
OFF

TUESDAY
BIKING: 3h. 3h. medium pace up to 150bpm.

WEDNESDAY

SWIMMING: 3.500m 3.500m = 75% free style + 25% other strokes Intensity: Easy.	WEIGHTS + RUNNING: Weights: You need to follow the exercises of the routine 2. Execute 15 repetitions per exercise and switcht to the next exercise, and repeat the routine 3 times. Really short rest between exercises. This time, once you finish the 3 times, run 55' at easy pace = 7'43" / mile.

THURSDAY

BIKING: 3h
Nice and easy biking. (135bpm max) with
S.T 2: : 2 x 10' (20"L.leg + 20" R.leg) with 75% tension.
5' n&e .
20' (30" sprint + 1'30" nice and easy) all them at 75%.
Cool down till you ride the 3h.

FRIDAY

SWIMMING: (no more than 1h 10'.) 3.500m Intensity: Easy.	RUNNING: 1h15' 1h15' easy run = 7'43"/ mile

SATURDAY

SATURDAY WORKOUT = BIKING + RUN (key workout): 100miles + track
*Tempo ride for 100miles + right after
1 x 1600m in 6:50.8 to 7:06
1 x 1200m in between 5:01 to 5:14
1 x 800m in between 3:11 to 3:20
1 x 400m in between 1:34 to 1:38
1 x 200m in between 40 to 44
Rest as much as you need in order to make the times.

SUNDAY

SWIM TO RUN: 5.000m. nice and easy swim. 1h 30' at 7'43"/ mile pace.	TOTAL TIME: 20h40'

NOTES:
1.- Second week of volume.
2.- *Saturday. This is the key workout, if you have to miss a workout, don't miss this one. Get a 100 miles loop where you don't have to stop for traffic lights or stop signs too often, ride it as fast as you can but steady pace, allways smooh and at constant. Try to stop for water and foot only when necesary. Right after drive to a track field (5' transition) and run the track workout, at 95% max effort, resting as much as you need in order to make the times. Even if that means you need to rest 5' in between intervals.
3.- Sunday will be your long swim day + running.
4.- From now on your base running pace is 7'43"/mile

WEEK NUM. 3 FROM MAY 23 TO 29
2.005 (3 rd. Week microcycle I):

MONDAY
OFF

TUESDAY
BIKING: 3h. 3h. medium pace up to 150bpm.

WEDNESDAY

SWIMMING: 3.500m Note: Try to breack them in shorter sets (up to 500m resting 10" in between) 3.500m = 75% free style + 25% other strokes Intensity: Easy.	WEIGHTS + RUNNING: Weights: You need to follow the exercises of the routine 3. Execute 15 repetitions per exercise and switcht to the next exercise, and repeat the routine 3 times. Really short rest between exercises. This time, once you finish the 3 times, run 1h at easy pace = 7'24" / mile.

THURSDAY

BIKING: 3h
Nice and easy biking. (135bpm max) with
S.T 3: : 2 x 10' (20"L.leg + 20" R.leg) with 75% tension.
5' n&e .
20' (1'30" race pace + 30" sprint + 1'30" nice and easy) all them at 75%.
10' (1' standing up at 90% tension and really slow cadence + 1' seated and at race pace at 60% tension)
Cool down till you ride the 3h.

FRIDAY

SWIMMING: (no more than 1h 10'.) 3.500m Intensity: Easy.	RUNNING: 1h15' 1h15' easy run = 7'24"/ mile

SATURDAY

SATURDAY WORKOUT = BIKING + RUN (key workout): 100miles + track
*Tempo ride for 100miles + right after
1 x 1600m in 6:50.8 to 7:06
1 x 200m in between 40 to 44
1 x 2000m in between 8:44
1 x 200m in between 40 to 44
1 x 800m in between 3:10 to 3:15
1 x 200m in between 40 to 44
Rest as much as you need in order to make the times.

SUNDAY

SWIM TO RUN: 4.000m. nice and easy swim. 1h 45' at 8'00"/ mile pace.	TOTAL TIME: 21h.0

NOTES:
1.- Third week of volume. After this one rest week.
2.- *Saturday. This is the key workout, don't miss it.
3.- After last Saturday's track workout, I really think we can increase your run workouts pace, so far this week down to 7'24" pace.

WEEK NUM. 4 FROM MAY 30 TO 6 2.005 (rest week):

MONDAY
OFF

TUESDAY
SWIMMING: 1.500m Note: Remember to try to breack them in shorter sets (up to 500m resting 10" in between) 1.500m = 75% free style + 25% other strokes Intensity: Easy

WEDNESDAY
RUNNING: Nice and easy 45' run Intensity: Low.

THURSDAY
BIKING: 1h30 Nice and easy biking. (155bpm max) No specific workouts, take it easy.

FRIDAY
SWIMMING: 1.500m 1.500m = 75% free style + 25% other strokes Intensity: Easy

SATURDAY
BIKING + RUNNING (SESSION 1): 3h +35' Team (2 cyvlist) time trial + 35' track workout

SUNDAY	
OFF	TOTAL TIME: 7h.

NOTES:
1.- Recovering week.
2.- This week is designed for you to rest. Don't do anything extra!!
3.- Saturday. Time trial by teams.

WEEK NUM. 5 FROM JUNE 7 TO 12 2.005
(1frst. Week microcycle II):

MONDAY
OFF

TUESDAY
BIKING: 3h 3h. easy medium ride up to 150bpm.

WEDNESDAY	
SWIMMING: 3.000m Note: Remember to try to breack them in shorter sets (up to 500m resting 10" in between) 3.000m = 75% free style + 25% other strokes Intensity: Easy	WEIGHTS + RUNNING: Weights: You need to follow the exercises of the routine 1. Execute 15 repetitions per exercise and switcht to the next exercise, and repeat the routine 2 times. Really short rest between exercises. This time, once you finish the 3 times, run 1h10'at easy pace = 7:24 to 7:43/ mile.

THURSDAY
BIKING: 3h Nice and easy biking. (135bpm max) with S.T 4: : 2 x 10' (1'L.leg + 1' R.leg) with 65% tension. 5' n&e . 20' (30" race pace + 30" over race pace + 30" sprint + 1'30" nice and easy) all them at 75%. 10' (1' standing up at really easy 20% tension and really fast cadence + 1' seated at 70% tension) Cool down till you ride the 3h.

FRIDAY
SWIMMING: (no more than 1h.) 2.500m Intensity: Easy.

SATURDAY
BIKING + RUN (key workout): 100miles + track *Tempo ride for 100miles + right after 3 x 1 x 800m in between 3:11 to 3:20 1 x 400m in between 1:25 to 1:34 1 x 200m in between 40 to 44" This time there is no rest. You just jogg really slow for 200m.

SUNDAY	
SWIMMING + RUNNING: 2.500m. nice and easy swim + 45' at 140bpm, (no mather what pace you are running at).	TOTAL TIME: 18h25'.

NOTES:
1.- First week of volume.
2.- Some changes. As I told you already, your day for a long run is going to be on Tuesdays in state of Sundays. That will give you more time to recover from Saturday, you will start with a "short" 1h10' run after weights. Second change is your run intervals after the bike on Saturday. Untill last week you always rested as long as you needed to make the times, from now on, we know you can make the times, so you will star cutting down rest time. This week you just have 200m jogg/walk before you start another interval.
3.- Important: Saturday, is the key day. All week needs to be focusing towards Saturday. In other words. Saturday workouts are the ones are going to help you to do it well at the IM. The rest of the week's workout are going to help you to do the Saturday's workouts as planned.
4.- As you can see also, no much swim this week. That is ok.

WEEK NUM. 6 FROM JUNE 13 TO 19 2.005:

MONDAY
OFF

TUESDAY	
BIKING: 2h30' 2h30'. easy medium ride up to 150bpm.	SWIMMING: 1.500m Note: Remember to try to breack them in shorter sets (up to 500m resting 10" in between) 1.500m = 75% free style + 25% other strokes Intensity: Easy

WEDNESDAY
WEIGHTS + RUNNING: Weights: You need to follow the exercises of the routine 2. Execute 15 repetitions per exercise and switcht to the next exercise, and repeat the routine 3 times. Really short rest between exercises. This time, once you finish the 3 times, run 1h45'at easy pace = 7:24 to 7:43/ mile

THURSDAY
BIKING: 3h Nice and easy biking. (155bpm max) with S.T 16: : 2 x 10' (1'L.leg + 1' R.leg) with 65% tension. 5' n&e . 2 X 1'hard seating down 2' easy seating down 2' hard standing up 2' easy standing up 3' hard seating down 2' easy seating down 4' hard out of the saddle 2' easy out of the saddle Cool down till you ride the 3h.

FRIDAY
SWIMMING: (no more than 1h.) 2.500m Intensity: Easy.

SATURDAY
BIKING + RUN (key workout): 112miles + track *Tempo ride for 112miles + right after 3 x 3miles in 6:50 to 7:06 This time there is no rest. You just jogg really slow for 800m.

SUNDAY	
SWIMMING + RUNNING: 3.000m. nice and easy swim + 50' at 140bpm, (no mather what pace you are running at).	TOTAL TIME: 19h.

NOTES:
1.- Second week of volume. You just have 1 more week of volume after this one, then 1 week of active recovering, and 3 more weeks of specificworkouts and tapering. You are almost there.
2.- Some changes. You will bike shorter on Tuesdays but you will swim too. The reasson for that is becouse I want you run long once a week.
3.- As I told you Saturday is the key workout. That is the most important workout of the week. The second most important is Wednesday's long run after the weights. In that day you need to run the distance at the pace I ask you, too slow won't help you that much. In other words, if you want to run the marathon after the bike in 3h15' we need to make sure we teach your body to run at that pace for that long, that is the mission of the Wednesday's run. Swimming: So far is not that important, we didin't work in your swim yet but we will. At the moment just try to improve your technique as much as possible before we start working on specific workouts. Swimming is your nice and aerobic workout.
3.- Biking. From now on your long rides are 112miles. Sorry ☹
4.- Notice that we are not training that many hours, but lots of quality workouts.

WEEK NUM. 7 FROM JUNE 20 TO 26 2.005:

MONDAY
OFF

TUESDAY	
BIKING: 2h 2h. easy medium ride up to 150bpm.	SWIMMING: 1.500m Note: Remember to try to breack them in shorter sets (up to 500m resting 10" in between) 1.500m = 75% free style + 25% other strokes Intensity: Easy

WEDNESDAY
RUNNING: 2h15'at easy pace = 7:24 to 7:43/ mile.

THURSDAY
BIKING: 1h30 Nice and easy biking. (155bpm max) No specific workouts, take it easy.

FRIDAY
SWIMMING: (no more than 1h.) 2.500m Intensity: Easy.

SATURDAY
BIKING : Brutal 200miles

SUNDAY	
SWIMMING : 2.500m at easy pace.	TOTAL TIME: 20h.

NOTES:

1.- Third and last week of volume phase. You are almost there.

2.- This week is designed for you to get rested enough to Saturday's ride. Try to do a intens work on that ride.

3.- O.K Next week rest week and we get into the last phase, where we need to put everything together. It would be good if for the following Saturdays July 3rd, 10 and 17th you could join us for a specific workouts. They are only about 4h duration, and they will be a key for your tune up. We will be a lot of athletes training for similars events.

WEEK NUM. 8 FROM JUNE 27 TO 3 2.005:

MONDAY
OFF

TUESDAY
SWIMMING: 1.500m Note: Remember to try to breack them in shorter sets (up to 500m resting 10" in between) 1.500m = 75% free style + 25% other strokes Intensity: Easy

WEDNESDAY
OFF.

THURSDAY
BIKING: 1h30 Nice and easy biking. (155bpm max) No specific workouts, take it easy.

FRIDAY
RUNNING: Nice and easy 45' run Intensity: Low

SATURDAY
BIKING + RUNNING (SESSION 1): 3h +35' Team (2 cyvlist) time trial + 35' track workout

SUNDAY	
OFF	TOTAL TIME: 6h25'.

MONDAY	
SWIMMING	2.500m at easy pace

NOTES:
1.- Recovering week.
2.- This week is designed for you to rest. Don't do anything extra!!
3.- Saturday. Time trial by teams.

WEEK NUM. 9 FROM JULY 4 TO 10 2.005:

MONDAY	
OFF	
TUESDAY	

BIKING: 2h
2h. easy medium ride up to 150bpm.
	SWIMMING:
	Workout 1: W.U 500m +
	+ 5 x 100m free in 1'45"/1'40"/1'35"/1'30"/1'25"
	100 nice and easy in between each 100m +
	  30"rest.
	+ 5 x 100m free = 4 x (half length moderate/
	  half length sprint)
	100 nice and easy in between each 100m +
	  30"rest.
	+ 10 x 25m = (half length sprint + stop in the
	  midle of the pool +sprint the rest of the
	  length) (45" rest)
	All of them starting from the wall. No diving.
	250m Cool down

WEDNESDAY	

WEIGHTS :
Weights: You need to follow the
  exercises of the routine 2. Execute
  15 repetitions per exercise and
  switcht to the next exercise, and
  repeat the routine 3 times. Really
  short rest between exercises. No
  run after!
	RUNNING:
	2h30'at easy pace = 7:24 to 7:43/ mile.

THURSDAY	
BIKING: 2h Nice and easy biking. (155bpm max) No specific workouts, take it easy.	
FRIDAY	
SWIMMING: (no more than 1h.30) 4.000m Long sets of up to 400m. Intensity: Easy.	
SATURDAY	
BIKING + RUN (key workout): 100miles + track *Tempo ride for 100miles + right after 5k in 20:00	
SUNDAY	

SWIMMING + RUNNING:
2.500m. nice and easy swim + 45'
  at 140bpm, (no mather what pace
  you are running at).
	TOTAL TIME: 17h.50'

NOTES:
1.- First week of volume. You are almost there. This is last week of real hard work, eventhough it is only 17h50'
2.- You have a long run on Wednesday, your last long one.
3.- Saturday (all out), is the key workout. Get a loop of 100miles, and try to ride them as hard as possible, with only 2 or 3 stops, for water and food. It is very important you try your best to go as fast as possible, and time it, becouse it would give me an idea how fast you can do the Ironman, and we will be able to plan accordingly.
4.- Sunday is mostly a recovering day.

WEEK NUM. 10 FROM JULY 11 TO 17 2.005:

MONDAY
OFF

TUESDAY
SWIMMING: 3.000m Intensity: Easy

WEDNESDAY	
BIKING + TRACK: 2:30'. Nice and easy biking up to only 140bpm	TRACK WORKOUT: 2 x 2.000m in 8'37" TO 8'52" (rest as long as you need to repeat the interval at the same pace!!!)

THURSDAY
OFF

FRIDAY	
SWIMMING: 2.000m =1h10' Intensity: Easy (Up to 75% of max H.R)	RUNNING: 6 miles really nice and easy. Don't even look at your watch and go by feelings.

SATURDAY
SWIMMING + BIKING (key workout): _4.000m swim at race pace + 3h biking.

SUNDAY	
SWIMMING + RUNNING: 2.000m. nice and easy swim + 45'running at 140bpm, (no mather what pace you are running at).	TOTAL TIME: 11h.45'

NOTES:
1.- Tapering week 1. Everything needs to be easy except the 1 speed workouts, and tempo ride on Saturday.
2.- Saturday. We will workout together. Warm up for about 45' + group time trial + cool down.

WEEK NUM. 11 FROM JULY 18 TO 24 2.005:

MONDAY
OFF
TUESDAY
BIKING: 2h. Nice and easy biking 2 hours.
WEDNESDAY
OFF
THURSDAY
BIKING: 2h. 2h really easy to the bike length.
FRIDAY
RUNNING : Up to 8km really easy at the run length
SATURDAY
SWIMMING: 1000m at the start line.
SUNDAY

IRONMAN LAKE PLACID 10h42' and qualifyed for Hawaii Ironman World Championship.	TOTAL TIME: 5h.30' + Race

NOTES:
1.- Mark, now is all about resting. There isn't anything in the next week you can do to improve your fitness. The most important thing now is get your levels of stress and anxiety down. You can run a litle bit on Saturday if you feel like, but really slow. During this week don't eat, or do anythink different than the other weeks, last minute changes usualy never work.

10 WEEKS TRAINING FOR A 12 TO 13 HOURS IRONMAN:

Athlete: Mark Kelley (Male)
Age: 47
Weight: 185lbs to 175lbs
Status: Married
Profesion: CEO
Base training prior to the program: 10h to 13h. a week
Time available for training: 18 hours a week conditioned by work
His best sport: Running
Groups: Master swim at P.A.C, 1h. Organized tri-training and Saturday ride with a group of friends.
Goal for the seasson: Finish an Ironman

WEEK NUM. 1 FROM JUNE 16 TO 22 2.008:

MONDAY
OFF

TUESDAY
BIKE: 2h.30 S.W 3 = HILLS 6 x TORREY PINES OUTSIDE ROAD (+ - 1km). 1frst. Tempo climb. Always same pace (up to 170bpm) 2nd. Slow climb long gear. The longest/hardest gear you can ride for the entired climb. (160bpm) 3rd. Spinning climb. Shortest gear fast cadence. (150bpm) 4th. Tempo climb again. 5th. One leg climb. ½ of the climb w/right leg, ½ w/left leg. 6th. Accelerations. 1' easy 20" fast al the way to the top. 15' Cool Down.

WEDNESDAY	
SWIMMING: 2.000y 2.000 yards nice and easy swim.	RUNNING: 1h easy run (140bpm max)

THURSDAY	
WEIGHTS + RUNNING: Follow the weights workout "routine 2". Repeat the whole workout 3 times. Right after 20' runing at 7':24" to 7':43" pace per mile..	SWIMMING: Swim lesson with carles 1h.

FRIDAY
TRI-TRAINING: It is time to push hard!

SATURDAY
BIKE + RUN: 3h + 20' " Nice and easy ride (135bpm max) + right after 20' at 7'24" to 7'43

SUNDAY	
SWIM TO RUN: 3.500m (no more than 1h.20'), right after your long run 1h40' (140bpm max)	TOTAL TIME: 14h55

NOTES:
1.- Third volume week of the second micro-cycle of the specific training phase. We have some key days: 1.- Tuesday biking. Try to ride exactly as it is.
2.- Thursday's swim lesson, just technique.
3.- Friday's tri training. Your speed workout of the week.
4.- The run after the bike at 7:24 to 7:43. It is really important you try to run that long at that pace. I reader you run shorter but at that pace, that longer but slower.

WEEK NUM. 2 FROM JUNE 23 TO 29 2.008:

MONDAY
OFF

TUESDAY
BIKING: (on the road or on the turbo training) 1h 30' with specific bike workout . S.W 1: 10' (30" pedaling only r.leg +30" l. leg) (specific workout) + 1' hard + 1' easy + 2' hard + 1'easy + 3' hard + 1'easy +2' hard +1' easy + 1'hard + 1'easy + Cool down Hard= up to 90%

WEDNESDAY
MASTERS' SWIM: 1.500y Whatever they ask you. No more than 1.500y. Intensity: Easy(H.R Max 70%)

THURSDAY
OFF

FRIDAY
TRI-TRAINING: Whatever they asck you. Time to give your best.

SATURDAY
SATURDAY WORKOUT = 2h 45'hours 2h biking (153 bpm) + 2.5miles easy.

SUNDAY	
RUNNING + STRETCHING: 1h easy run + 1h stretching Intensity : Everything low (HR Max 70%)	TOTAL: 7:00h.+ 1h stretching

NOTES:
1.- As you can see this is your active recovering week. You did a awesome job last 3 week so now is time for your body to recover and get stronger. So don't do more that what it is in the schedule.
2.-Friday: All out

WEEK NUM. 3 FROM JUNE 30 TO 6 2.008:

MONDAY
OFF

TUESDAY
BIKING: 3h Nice and easy biking. (135bpm max) with <u>S.W 2:</u> With the longest/hardest gear possible 12' (2'R leg + 2'L.leg) 8' (1'R leg + 1'L.leg) 5' (30"R leg + 30"L.leg) 3' (15"R leg + 15"L.leg) Cool down till you ride the 3h.

WEDNESDAY	
MASTERS' SWIM: 3.000y Whatever they ask you. No more than 3.000y. Intensity: Easy(H.R Max 70%)	TRACK: 1h. Warm up 15' then 4 X 200m in 50" 400m in 1'45" 400m in 1'45" 200m in 50" 200m in 50" Rest 1m walk in between intervals. Cool down 10'

THURSDAY
RUNNING: 1h. Easy run Intensity: Easy, up to 130bpm!!

FRIDAY
TRI-TRAINING: Whatever they asck you. Time to give your best.

SATURDAY
SATURDAY WORKOUT = 4h 30'hours 4h biking (153 bpm Max) + 3 miles in 25'55" + cool down.

SUNDAY	
SWIMMING + RUNNING + STRETCHING: 1.500y swimming really easy then right after your long run of the week. 1h30 easy run + 1h stretching Intensity : Everything low (HR Max 155bpm)	TOTAL: 14h5'.+ 1h stretching

NOTES:
1.- First week of volume of another micro-cycle. More specific workouts. You have track for first time this week, so be careful with injuries.
2.- I know some times is hard, but it would be good for you if you swim with masters time to time, it is a way to go faster without feelling it so much.

WEEK NUM. 4 FROM JULY 7 TO 13 2.008:

MONDAY	
OFF	
TUESDAY	
BIKING: 3h. nice and easy ride. Intensity: up to 135bpm.	TRACK: (Specific workout for California) 3 x (400m in 1'35"+ 600m in 2'20"+ 1.000m in 3'55") all with 100m walk in between.
WEDNESDAY	

MASTERS' SWIM: 3.000y
Whatever they ask you. No more than
  3.000y.
Intensity: Easy(H.R Max 70%)
	WEIGHTS + RUNNING:
	Follow the weights workout "routine 2".
	  Repeat the whole workout 3 times.
	Right after 20' runing nice and easy.

THURSDAY	
BIKING: 3h Nice and easy biking. (135bpm max) with S.W 3: 6 x (1'R. Leg + 1' L.Leg + 2' really hard, up to 175bpm.) + 10' nice and easy + 6' at race pace (170bpm) Cool down till you ride the 3h.	
FRIDAY	
TRI-TRAINING: Whatever they asck you. Time to give your best.	
SATURDAY	
SATURDAY WORKOUT = 3hours + run 3h biking (153 bpm Max) + 2 miles nice and easy	
SUNDAY	
SANDIEGUITO ½ MARATHON:	TOTAL: 13h35'.+ Race

NOTES:
  1.- Second week of volume. More specific workouts.
  2.- Track: I am really happy how it went last week. Your times were
      more than good. This time try to run track right after the biking
      if that is possible for you. It will give you the same feeling than in
      the race day.
  3.-San Dieguito ½ marathon. Unfortunatly you will have to run this
      race feeling tired from the week training, but it is a good fitness
      test.

WEEK NUM. 5 FROM JULY 14 TO 20 2.008:

MONDAY
OFF

TUESDAY
BIKING:

WEDNESDAY
MASTERS' SWIM: 3.000y Whatever they ask you. No more than 3.000y. Intensity: Easy(H.R Max 70%)

THURSDAY	
BIKING: 3h Nice and easy biking. (145bpm max)	TRACK: (Specific workout for California) 6 x 1000m in 4'15" to 4'20". 400m rest in between.

FRIDAY
TRI-TRAINNING: Whatever they asck you. You don't need to push hard this time.

SATURDAY
SATURDAY WORKOUT = 4hours + run 4h biking (153 bpm Max) + 3 miles in 24'

SUNDAY	
SWIMMING +RUNNING: 1h 10'+ 1h45' 3.000y, nice and easy (not longer than 1h10') Nice and easy run up to 140bpm max.	TOTAL: 16h45'

NOTES:
1.-Third week of volume. More specific workouts. Even though you have Monday off, Tuesday easy bike, and Wednesday easy swim, it is an almost 17h week. But It is your last very long week. Next week rest.
2.- Track: It is going to hurt ;-)
3.- Saturday ride and Sunday run, it would be good if you find someone or group to go with.

WEEK NUM. 6 FROM JULY 21 TO 27 2.005:

MONDAY
OFF
TUESDAY
TRACK WORKOUT: 1h15' Intensity moderate!
WEDNESDAY
SWIMMING: 1h really easy. Time to work on your technique again.
THURSDAY
RUNNING: 1h Intensity: Up to 135bpm.
FRIDAY
BIKE WORKOUT: 1h15' Intensity: Moderate to low.
SATURDAY
OFF
SUNDAY

SWIMMING + RUNNING: 1.000m. nice and easy swim + 1h= 6miles or running at 140bpm.	TOTAL TIME: 6h.10'

NOTES: 1.- Rest week. . Please, don't do more of what is in the schedule, we are way to close to the race, injuries or overtraining would be terrible at this point.

WEEK NUM. 7 FROM JULY 28 TO 3 2.008:

MONDAY
OFF
TUESDAY
BIKING: 3h Nice and easy biking. (135bpm max) with: With the longest/hardest gear possible 12' (2'R leg + 2'L.leg) 8' (1'R leg + 1'L.leg) 5' (30"R leg + 30"L.leg) 3' (15"R leg + 15"L.leg)
WEDNESDAY

SWIMMING: (no more than 1h10') 3.500m Intensity: Easy.	RUNNING: 45' Nice and easy (140bpm max)

THURSDAY
BIKING: 3h Nice and easy biking. (140bpm max)
FRIDAY

SWIMMING: (no more than 1h10'.) 3.500m Intensity: Easy.	WEIGHTS + RUNNING: Weights: You need to follow the exercises of the routine 1. Execute 15 repetitions per exercise and switcht to the next exercise, and repeat the routine 3 times. Really short rest between exercises. This time, each time you finish a circuit (3 of them) you need to run 1 mile on the treadmill in 5'45".

SATURDAY
BIKE + RUN: 4h + 45' 4h easy biking (135bpm max). Right after 45' easy run (140bpm max)
SUNDAY

SWIM TO RUN: 2.500m (no more than 50'), right after your long run 1h45' (140bpm max)	TOTAL TIME: 17h50'

NOTES:
1.- First week of volume for IM Canada
2.- Swimming. Just go the distance
3.- Super important; respect intensities or you may not make it to August 24th in proper shape.

WEEK NUM. 8 FROM AUGUST 4 TO 10 2.008:

MONDAY
OFF

TUESDAY
BIKING: 3h nice and easy biking (135bpm max) With: S.W 4: . 9' (45"'R. Leg + 45" L.Leg) + (10' nice and easy in between sets) 1' 4rd longest gear at 90rpm (more or less) 1' 3rd longest gear at 90rpm + 3 x 1' 2nd longest gear at 80rpm 1' Longest gear possible at 75rpm 1' Longest gear possible standing up and 65rpm (max. effort) = 175bpm + Cool down

WEDNESDAY	
SWIMMING: (no more than 1h10') 3.500m Intensity: Easy.	WEIGHTS + RUNNING: Weights: You need to follow the exercises of the routine 3. Execute 15 repetitions per exercise and switcht to the next exercise, and repeat the routine 3 times. Really short rest between exercises. This time, each time you finish a circuit (3 of them) you need to run 1 mile on the treadmill in 5'50".

THURSDAY
BIKING: 3h Nice and easy biking. (140bpm max)

FRIDAY	
SWIMMING: (no more than 1h10'.) 3.500m With this intervals 10 x 100m free leaving the wall in: 2' 1'55" 1'40" 1'50" 1'50" 1'40" 1'55' 1'45 1'45" 2' Intensity: Easy for the rest of the workout.	RUNNING: 1h Nice and easy (140bpm max)

SATURDAY	

SATURDAY WORKOUT = 5hours +
   TRACK
3h biking (153 bpm Max) + track
	TRACK: (Specific workout for IM Canada)
	3 x (400m in 1'30"+ 600m in 2'15"+ 1.000m
	   in 3'50") all with 100m walk in between.

SUNDAY	
SWIM TO RUN: 2.500m (no more than 1h.), right after your long run 1h55' (140bpm max)	TOTAL TIME: 18h30'

NOTES:
1.- Third week of volume.
2.- Tuesday bike workout supper important.
3.- We will repeat the same Saturday than last week.
4.- Friday Swimming. I would like to know if you could swim the set
    I ask you to swim of 10x 100m. And how hard it was for you.

WEEK NUM. 9 FROM AUGUST 11 TO 17 2.008:

MONDAY
OFF

TUESDAY
BIKING: 2h nice and easy biking (135bpm max) With: <u>S.W 5</u>: . W.U + 10' (20"'R. Leg + 20" L.Leg) Longest gear you have. + 20' (30"sprint + 1'30" easy) Longest gear you have. + Cool down

WEDNESDAY	
BIKING: 2h nice and easy biking (135bpm max) With: <u>S.W 5</u>: . W.U + 10' (20"'R. Leg + 20" L.Leg) Longest gear you have. + 20' (30"sprint + 1'30" easy) Longest gear you have. + Cool down	WEIGHTS + RUNNING: Weights: You need to follow the exercises of the routine 1. Execute 15 repetitions per exercise and switcht to the next exercise, and repeat the routine 3 times. Really short rest between exercises. This time, each time you finish a circuit (3 of them) you need to run 1 mile on the treadmill in 5'45".

THURSDAY
OFF

FRIDAY			
SWIMMING: (no more than 1h10'.) 2.500m With this intervals 10 x 100m free leaving the wall in:	2'	1'40"	1'55'
	1'55"	1'40"	2'
	1'50"	1'45"	
	1'45"	1'50"	
	Intensity: Easy for the rest of the workout.		

SATURDAY	
SATURDAY WORKOUT = 3hours + TRACK 3h biking All out effort + track	TRACK: (Specific workout for IM Canada) 4 x 1.600m in 5'38". 400m rest in between.

SUNDAY	
OFF	TOTAL TIME: 9h30'

NOTES:
1.- Third week of volume and last. This week though is all about speed, don't go over the distance.
2.- Tuesday bike workout. Try on those 30" sprint, to go as hard as possible.
3.- Saturday track: It is going to be hard ;)
4.- Friday Swimming we try it again.

WEEK NUM. 10 FROM AUGUST 18 TO 24 2.008:

MONDAY	
OFF	
TUESDAY	
BIKING: 2h. Nice and easy biking 2 hours.	
WEDNESDAY	
OFF	
THURSDAY	
BIKING: 2h. 2h really easy to the bike length.	
FRIDAY	
RUNNING : Up to 8km really easy at the run legth	
SATURDAY	
SWIMMING: 1000m at the start line.	
SUNDAY	
IRONMAN CANADA Total Time = 12h14'	TOTAL TIME: 5h.30' + Race

NOTES:

1.- Mark, now is all about resting. There isn't anything in the this week you can do to improve your fitness. The most important thing now is get your levels of stress as low as possible, relax the work is done, you are ready. Feel confidend.You can run a litle bit on Saturday if you feel like, but really slow. During this week don't eat, or do anythink different than the other weeks, last minute changes usualy never work.

HALF IRONMAN DISTANCE:

10 WEEKS TRAINING FOR A 4h15 TO 4h45 HOURS HALF IRONMAN:

Athlete: Carlos Civit
Age: 30
Weight: 162,8 to 165lbs
Status: Single
Profesion: Former Pro. Triathlete, personal trainer and coach.
Base training prior to the program: 10 weeks averaging 20h a week
Time available for training: Schedule conditioned by work. Blocks of 3 to 4h training sessions, up to 6 hours a day
His best sport: Swimming/running
Groups: Majority of training alone.

Carlos Civit

WEEK NUM. 1 FROM FEBRUARY 27 TO 3 1999:

MONDAY
OFF

TUESDAY

BIKING:
3h nice and easy biking (135bpm max)
With: S.T 1: .
W.U + 10' (20'''R. Leg + 20'' L.Leg) Longest gear you have.
+ 20' (30''sprint + 1'30'' easy) Longest gear you have.
+ Cool down

WEDNESDAY

SWIMMING: (no more than 1h10')
3.500m
Intensity: Easy.

WEIGHTS + RUNNING:
Weights: You need to follow the exercises of the routine 1. Execute 15 repetitions per exercise and switcht to the next exercise, and repeat the routine 3 times. Really short rest between exercises. This time, each time you finish a circuit (3 of them) you need to run 1 mile on the treadmill in 5'45''.

THURSDAY

BIKING: 3h15'
Nice and easy biking. (140bpm max)

FRIDAY

SWIMMING 3.500m : (no more than 1h10'.)
With this interval 10 x 100m free leaving the wall in: 1'45'' 1'30''

1'40''	1'35''	1'30''
1'25''	1'35''	1'40'
1'45''	1'50''	

Intensity: Easy for the rest of the workout.

RUNNING:
1h 15' Nice and easy (140bpm max)
7' to 7'15''/ mile

SATURDAY

SATURDAY WORKOUT = 3hours 30'+ TRACK
3h 30' biking (153 bpm Max) + track

TRACK: (Specific workout for ½ IM St. Croix)
4 x 1.600m in 5'38''. 400m rest in between.

SUNDAY

SWIM TO RUN:
2.500m (no more than 1h.), right after your long run 2h (140bpm max)

TOTAL TIME: 18h45'

NOTES:
1.- First week again of volume of your second micro-cycle.
2.- Tuesday bike workout. Try on those 30'' sprint, to go as hard as possible.
3.- Saturday track: It is going to be hard ; 4.- Please respect the intensities.

142

WEEK NUM. 2 FROM MARCH 4 TO 10 1999:

MONDAY
OFF

TUESDAY
BIKING: 3h nice and easy biking (135bpm max) With: <u>S.T 2</u>: W.U + 3 x 10' really hard. + 7' rest in between. + Cool down

WEDNESDAY	
SWIMMING: (no more than 1h10') 3.500m Intensity: Easy.	WEIGHTS + RUNNING: Weights: You need to follow the exercises of the routine 1. Execute 15 repetitions per exercise and switcht to the next exercise, and repeat the routine 1 3 times. Really short rest between exercises. This time, run 10' nice and easy after the each cicuit.

THURSDAY
BIKING: 3h30' Nice and easy biking. (140bpm max)

FRIDAY	
SWIMMING: (no more than 1h10'.) 3.500m Intensity: Easy.	RUNNING: 1h 15' Nice and easy (140bpm max) 6'55" to 7'/ mile

SATURDAY
SATURDAY WORKOUT = 4hours 30'+ Run 3h 30' biking (153 bpm Max) + run Race simulation 1

SUNDAY	
SWIM TO RUN: 2.500m (no more than 1h.), right after your long run 1h45' (140bpm max)	TOTAL TIME: 18h40'

NOTES:
1.- Second week of volume. Do as much as you can do without stressing out if there is something you are too tired to do it, we still have plenty of time to get you in awesome shape.

WEEK NUM. 3 FROM MARCH 11 TO 17 1999:

MONDAY
OFF

TUESDAY
BIKING: 3h Nice and easy biking. (140bpm max)

WEDNESDAY	
SWIMMING: (no more than 1h) 3.000m Intensity: Easy.	WEIGHTS + RUNNING: Weights: You need to follow the exercises of the routine 2. Execute 12reps on 1frst circuit, 10 on the second, 8 repetitions per exercise on the last one. Really short rest between exercises. This time, run 30' nice and easy at the end of the workout.

THURSDAY
BIKING: 3h nice and easy biking (135bpm max) With: S.T 3: : W.U + 10 x 1' really hard. + 7' rest in between. + Cool down

FRIDAY	
SWIMMING: (no more than 1h.) 3.000m Intensity: Easy.	RUNNING: 1h 15' Nice and easy (140bpm max) 6'45" to 7'/ mile

SATURDAY
SATURDAY WORKOUT = 4hours 30'+ 45'Run 4h 30' biking up to what you decide to ride that day + 45'run Intensity: Moderate to low

SUNDAY	
SWIM TO RUN: 3.500m (no more than 1h10'), right after your long run 1h45' (140bpm max)	TOTAL TIME: 18h40'

NOTES:
1.- Third week of volume.
2.- Weights. It is good time to time go down in reps. to be able to increase the weight. It is only once every 2 month.
3.- The entired week is at low to moderate intensity, with th exception of Thursday workout.

WEEK NUM. 4 FROM MARCH 18 TO 24 1999:

MONDAY
OFF

TUESDAY
BIKING: 2h S.T 4 45' wu + 2 x 2' hard (1'easy) 2 x 3' hard (1'easy) 2 x 4' hard (1'easy) + 30' Cool Down Nice and easy biking. (140bpm max)

WEDNESDAY
SWIMMING: (no more than 45') 2.000m Intensity: Easy.

THURSDAY
WEIGHTS + RUNNING: Weights: You need to follow the exercises of the routine 3. Execute 12reps on 1frst circuit, 10 on the second, 8 repetitions per exercise on the last one. Really short rest between exercises. This time, run 45' nice and easy at the end of the workout.

FRIDAY
OFF

SATURDAY
RUN: 1h30' 1h30' easy run (HRMax 135bpm)

SUNDAY	
SWIM TO BIKE: 1.500m (no more than 35'), right after 2h nice and easy biking (150bpm max)	TOTAL TIME: 8h20'

NOTES:
1.- Finally a rest week! Take it as it is. All the workouts have to be easy. Remember that the goal of this week is to get ready for next micro-cycle.
2.- Weights: Keep still low rep. But try to increas the weight.

WEEK NUM. 5 FROM MARCH 25 TO 31 1999:

MONDAY
OFF

TUESDAY
BIKING: 3h Nice and easy biking. (140bpm max)

WEDNESDAY	
SWIMMING: 3.000m 3.000m Intensity: Easy.	WEIGHTS + RUNNING: Weights: You need to follow the exercises of the routine 3. Execute 15 repetitions per exercise and switcht to the next exercise, and repeat the routine 3 times. Really short rest between exercises. This time, once you finish the 3 times, run 45' at easy pace.

THURSDAY
BIKING: 3h Nice and easy biking. (135bpm max) with S.T 5: 6 x (1'R. Leg + 1' L.Leg + 2' really hard, up to 175bpm.) + 10' nice and easy + 4 x 6' at race pace (160bpm?)with 10" sprint every1' 10' easy pace in between the two sets. Cool down till you ride the 3h.

FRIDAY	
SWIMMING: (no more than 1h.) 3.000m Intensity: Easy.	RUNNING: 1h 15' From now on Thursday's run will be always your tempo run. This pace is 6'40"/mile. So 1h15' at 6'50"/mile

SATURDAY
SATURDAY WORKOUT = 4hours 30'+ 35'Run 3h 30' biking nice and easy + 35'run easy Intensity: Moderate to low

SUNDAY	
SWIM TO RUN: 2.000m at race pace = 30'(for the 2000m) right after, your long run 1h45' (140bpm max)	TOTAL TIME: 17h50'

NOTES:
1.- First week of volume.
2.- Thursdays. Your tempo biking.
3.- Fridays. Your tempo running.
4.- Sunday. Your tempo swimming.
5.- Respect intensities, or you will be too tired to make your tempo workouts.
6.- Every week you will workout less and less, resting more and more, but you have some workouts that are important you don't miss, and they are the tempo ones.

WEEK NUM. 6 FROM APRIL 1 TO 7 1999:

MONDAY
OFF

TUESDAY
BIKING: 3h Tempo ride. (160bpm max)

WEDNESDAY	
SWIMMING: 2.500m 3.000m Intensity: Easy.	WEIGHTS + RUNNING: Weights: You need to follow the exercises of the routine 1. Execute 15 repetitions per exercise and switcht to the next exercise, and repeat the routine 3 times. Really short rest between exercises. This time, once you finish the 3 times, run 35' at easy pace = 8'40" to 9'/ mile.

THURSDAY
BIKING: 2h30' Nice and easy biking. (135bpm max) with S.T 6: : W.U

+ 1 x 7' race pace. 2'rest	+ 2 x 6' 2'rest
+ 4 x 4' 1'rest	+ 3 x 5' 2'rest
+ 6'x 2' 1'rest	+ 5 x 3' 1'rest

Cool down till you ride the 3h.

FRIDAY	
SWIMMING: (no more than 1h.) 3.000m Intensity: Easy.	RUNNING: 1h45' 1h. 45' easy run this time = 6'40" to 7'/ mile

SATURDAY
SATURDAY WORKOUT = 4hours 30'+ track Run 3h 30' biking nice and easy = 21m/h average +

1 x 1.600m in 6'00" to 6'10"	1 x 1.200m in 4'20" to 4'00"
1 x 800m in 2:40" to 2'50"	1 x 400m in 1'20" to 1'25"
1 x 200m in 36" to 40"	

Cool down
Intensity: Moderate to low on the bike, whatever it takes on the run.

SUNDAY	
SWIM TO RUN: 50' 2.000m at race simulation = w.u 600m 100m in 1'20" (rest 30") 100m in 1'18" (rest 32") 100m in 1'16" (rest 34") 100m in 1'12" (rest 38") 100m in 1'08" (rest 42") 100m in 1'04" (rest 46") 100m in 1'08" (rest 42") 100m in 1'12" (rest 38") 100m in 1'16" (rest 34") 100m in 1'18" (rest 32") + 400m cool down + right after, your long run 1h40' = 8'38" to 10'/mile	TOTAL: 14h5'.+ 1h stretching

NOTES:
1.- Second week of volume.
2.-. Bike workout. It needs to be at really unconfortable pace, without getting to an anaerobic threshold.
3.- Fridays. Since you are going to do intervals on Saturday, this Friday is going to be an easy run in state of a tempo run.
4.- Sunday swim. This is a testt. So start warming up 600 follow up with the intervals with the appropiate rest. Swim as many as you can untill you don't make the times. Then cool down.

WEEK NUM. 7 FROM APRIL 8 TO 14 1999:

MONDAY	
OFF	

TUESDAY	
BIKING: 4h Tempo ride. (160bpm max)	RUNNING: 1h. 1h. easy run this time = 6'40" to 7'/ mile

WEDNESDAY	
SWIMMING: 2.500m 2.500m = 75% free style + 25% other strokes Intensity: Easy.	WEIGHTS + RUNNING: Weights: You need to follow the exercises of the routine 2. Execute 15 repetitions per exercise and switcht to the next exercise, and repeat the routine 3 times. Really short rest between exercises. This time, once you finish the 3 times, run 25' at easy pace = 8'40" to 9'/ mile.

THURSDAY
BIKING: 2h30' Nice and easy biking. (135bpm max) with S.T 7: : W.U 10 x (3' race pace+ 1' as fast as possible with the hardest gear possible) each set increase 2% the tension on your bike. + 4' really easy in between sets. Cool down till you ride the 2h30'.

FRIDAY	
SWIMMING: (no more than 1h.) 3.000m Intensity: Easy.	RUNNING: 1h. 1h. easy run this time = 6'40" to 7'/ mile

SATURDAY		
SATURDAY WORKOUT = 4hours 30'+ track Run 4h 30' biking nice and easy = 21.5m/h average + 12 x 400m		
In 1'14" 3' rest	In 1'22" 2'40" rest	In 1'20" 2' 30" rest
In 1'16" 3' rest	In 1' 24" 2'40" rest	In 1'18" 2'20" rest
In 1'18" 2'50" rest	In 1'24" 2'10" rest	In 1'16" 2'20" rest
In 1'20" 2'50" rest	In 1'22" 2'30" rest	In 1'14" 2' 10" rest
Cool down Intensity: Moderate to low on the bike, whatever it takes on the run.		

SUNDAY	
SWIM TO RUN: 2.000m. no more than 50' right after, your long run 1h30' = 7'38" to 8'/mile	TOTAL TIME: 17h15'

NOTES:
1.- Third week of volume.
2.-. Less time training more quality. You shouldn't feel tired but each
    week faster and faster.
3.- Saturday is a key workout, don't miss it. The bike should be by
    now a fast average pace.

WEEK NUM. 8 FROM APRIL 15 TO 21 1999:

MONDAY
OFF

TUESDAY
BIKING: 2h Nice and easy biking. (140bpm max)

WEDNESDAY	
SWIMMING: 2.500m 2.500m = 75% free style + 25% other strokes Intensity: Easy.	WEIGHTS + RUNNING: Weights: You need to follow the exercises of the routine 3. Execute 15 repetitions per exercise and switcht to the next exercise, and repeat the routine 3 times. Really short rest between exercises. This time, once you finish the 3 times, run 30' at easy pace = 8'40" to 9'/ mile.

THURSDAY
OFF

FRIDAY
SWIMMING: (no more than 1h.) 3.000m Intensity: Easy.

SATURDAY
SATURDAY WORKOUT = 3hours 30'+ track Run 3h 30' biking nice and easy = 21.5m/h average + 2 x 5000m both in 19' with 1600m nice and easy jogging Cool down Intensity: Moderate to low on the bike, whatever it takes on the run.

SUNDAY	
SWIM TO RUN: 2.000m. no more than 50'	TOTAL TIME: 10h5'

NOTES:
1.- Rest week. Take it as it is.
2.-. Saturday. Key workout, don't miss it.

WEEK NUM. 9 FROM APRIL 22 TO 28 1999:

MONDAY
OFF

TUESDAY
BIKING: 3h Nice and easy biking. (140bpm max)

WEDNESDAY	
SWIMMING: 2.500m 2.500m = 75% free style + 25% other strokes Intensity: Easy.	RUNNING: 1h. 1h easy run. Up to 140bpm

THURSDAY
OFF

FRIDAY
WEIGHTS + RUNNING: Weights: You need to follow the exercises of the routine 1. Execute 15 repetitions per exercise and switcht to the next exercise, and repeat the routine 3 times. Really short rest between exercises. This time, once you finish the 3 times, run 50' at easy pace = 8'40" to 9'/ mile.

SATURDAY
RACE SIMULATION: 1.500m swimming + 2h biking + 30' running Intensity: High

SUNDAY	
SWIM TO RUN: 2.000m. no more than 50' 1h. Nice and easy run. 140bpm	TOTAL TIME: 11h40'

NOTES:
1.- Tapering week.
2.- This week is pretty easy, and you neeed to take it this way.
3.- Saturday key workout, all out!!. Swim in your pool for 1.500m, right after take your bike and chose a 2 hours loop ride, without trafic lights and ride at race pace, right after 30' run at 6:24"/mile. Cool down.

WEEK NUM. 10 FROM APRIL 29 TO 5 1999:

MONDAY
OFF

TUESDAY
RUNNING: 50'   Nice and easy 50' run, to stretch out your legs.

WEDNESDAY
BIKING: 2h30 with specific bike workout.   Ride part of the race length +   S.T : W.U +   1 mile really fast + 10' easy +   2 miles really fast + 15' easy +   3 miles fast +   Cool down till 2h.

THURSDAY
SWIMMING: 45'   Nice and easy the entired swim length twice

FRIDAY
TRAVELLING FROM SPAIN TO CALIFORNIA

SATURDAY
TRAVELLING FROM SPAIN TO CALIFORNIA

SUNDAY	
½ IRONMAN WILDFLOWER Total time = 4h.40'	TOTAL TIME: 4:50'+ RACE

NOTES:
1.- Tapering week. Don't do more.

10 WEEKS TRAINING FOR A 5 TO 5:30 HOURS HALF IRONMAN:

Athlete: Peter Fuchs (Male)
Age: 35
Weight: 170lbs
Status: Married with kids
Profession: Sales representative.
Base training prior to the program: 10h to 13h. a week
Time available for training: 18 hours a week the most
His best sport: Swimming
Groups: Master swim at P.A.C, Tueasdays and Thursdays. Ride with a group of triathletes on Saturdays.
Goal for the seasson: Finish his first ½ Ironman

WEEK NUM 1. FROM JANUARY 26 TO 1 2.004:

MONDAY
SPINNING: 2 hours spinning back to back.   Intensity: Moderate (1fr class) to high (2nd class).

TUESDAY
OFF

WEDNESDAY
MASTERS' SWIM: Whatever they ask you.   Intensity: Moderate. (H.R Max 162b.p.m)

THURSDAY	
WEIGHTS: Weights for legs.+ 1 mile on the treadmill fast!.	RUNNING: 45' nice and easy run.

FRIDAY	
MASTERS' SWIM: Whatever they ask you. Intensity: High	SPINNING + RUNNING: 45' Spinning (up to 168 bpm) + 25' run as fast as possible (up to 172bpm).

SATURDAY
SATURDAY WORKOUT = 4h 45'hours   4h biking (153 bpm) + 45' moderate run (up to 162bpm)

SUNDAY	
RUNNING + SWIMMING: 1h30' Swim. + 1h.30' easy run Intensity : High in the pool, easy running. (HR Max 172bpm/ 155bpm)	TOTAL: 14:30h.

NOTES:
Tuesday. Work weights as hard as possible. :)
Swimming: On Friday you should swim at least 1.000y at 1'20"/100y
   pace
Saturday: The "long" day. Remember I am not here next Saturday,
   but you can go with that group of triathletes.

WEEK NUM 2 FROM FEBRUARY 2 TO 8 2.004:

MONDAY
OFF

TUESDAY

SPINNING: 2 hours spinning back to back. Intensity: Moderate (1fr class) to high (2nd class).	RUNNING: 45' nice and easy run.

WEDNESDAY
OFF

THURSDAY

MASTERS' SWIM:
Whatever they ask you.
Intensity: High

FRIDAY
OFF

SATURDAY

RUN:
40' Nice and easy with 10 x 50y up hill accelerations. 1' rest in between.

SUNDAY

SUN DIEGUITO 1/2 MARATHON

NOTES:
1.- The race morning: (1h30' before the race) 1 sanwitch of jamb with orange juice.
2.- Your first race! No excuses! you need to give your best from the start. The result will tell me what kind of shape you are right now and I will be able to adjust the training accordingly

WEEK NUM. 3 FROM FEBRUARY 9 TO 15
2.004 (last phase: specific workouts)

MONDAY
SPINNING: 2 hours spinning back to back. Intensity: Easy. Use this session to recover from the race.

TUESDAY
OFF

WEDNESDAY	
MASTERS' SWIM: Whatever they ask you. Intensity: Moderate. (H.R Max 162b.p.m)	RUNNING: 1h. Nice and easy run. Intensity: Low, up to 153bpm

THURSDAY	
RUNNING: 1h. Easy run Intensity: Moderate, up to 162bpm.	BIKING: (on the road or on the turbo training) 1h 30' with specific bike workout 1. S.B.W 1: 10' (30" pedaling only r.leg +30" l. leg) + 1' hard + 1' easy + 2' hard + 1'easy + 3' hard + 1'easy +2' hard +1' easy + 1'hard + 1'easy + Cool down

FRIDAY	
MASTERS' SWIM: At least 4.000yards. Whatever they ask you. Intensity: High	RUNNING: 1h. Nice and easy run. Intensity: Low, up to 153bpm

SATURDAY
SATURDAY WORKOUT = 4h 45'hours 4h biking (153 bpm) + 4k in 15'8" + cool down.

SUNDAY	
WEIGHTS + RUNNING + STRETCHING: 30' weights for legs + 1h30 easy run + 1h stretching Intensity : Everything low (HR Max 155bpm)	TOTAL: 15:50h.

NOTES:
1.- This week you start the specific training for the race. As you can see you have a specific bike workout on Thursday that you can do it or eather on the road or on the turbo training, but needs to be on your race bike.
2.- Tuesday: rest! Doesn't matter if you feel tired or not, rest.
3.- Saturday: We will go with the triathlete group and right after we will run 2.5 miles in 15'8" (goal pace for the race)

WEEK NUM. 4 FROM FEBRUARY 16 TO 22
2.004 (last phase: specific workouts)

MONDAY

SPINNING:
2 hours spinning back to back.
Intensity: Easy. Use this session to recover from the race.

TUESDAY

WEIGHTS: Weights for legs.+ 1 mile on the treadmill fast!.	TRACK: (Specific workout for California) 4 x 200m in 45" 8 x 400m in 1'30" 2 x 800m in 3' all with 100m walk in between. On Tuesday we start track again. This time we meet at La Costa Canyon High School Track.

WEDNESDAY

MASTERS' SWIM: Whatever they ask you. Intensity: Easy (H.R Max 162b.p.m)	RUNNING: 1h. Nice and easy run. Intensity: Low, up to 153bpm

THURSDAY

RUNNING: 1h. Easy run Intensity: Moderate, up to 162bpm.	BIKING: (on the road or on the turbo training) 1h 30' with specific bike workout 2. S.B.W 2: W.U + + 12' (2'R. Leg + 2' L.Leg) + 8' (1'R. Leg + 1' L.Leg) + 5' (30"R. Leg + 30" L.Leg) + 3' (15"R. Leg + 15" L.Leg) + Cool down

FRIDAY

MASTERS' SWIM: At least 4.000yards.
Whatever they ask you. With a test of 500y in 6'15"
Intensity: Moderate

SATURDAY

SATURDAY WORKOUT = 4h. 20'hours
4h biking (153 bpm) + 5k easy

SUNDAY

TORRY PINES 5K RUN: As hard as possible. Time stimate: none	TOTAL: 15:20h.

NOTES:
1.- Sunday race is just and speed workout session for you, don't get dessapinted with the times your legs will be tired and possibly "heavy"
2.- Remember, some times, more important than training is resting.

WEEK NUM. 5 FROM FEBRUARY 23 TO 29
2.004 (last phase: specific workouts)

MONDAY	
SPINNING: 1 hour spinning. Intensity: Easy. Use this session to recover from the weekend.	

TUESDAY	
WEIGHTS: No this week!	TRACK: (Specific workout for California) OFF

WEDNESDAY	
MASTERS' SWIM: Whatever they ask you. Try to swim as much as possible (5.000yards will be the ultimate!) Intensity: Easy (H.R Max 162b.p.m)	RUNNING: OFF

THURSDAY	
RUNNING + BIKING (Mini-brick):. 1h. Easy run + 1h spinning. Intensity: Moderate, up to 162bpm.	

FRIDAY	
MASTERS' SWIM: At least 4.000yards. Whatever they ask you. With a test (2nd) of 1.000y in 12'30" Intensity: Moderate	

SATURDAY	
SATURDAY WORKOUT = 4h. 30'hours 4h biking (153 bpm) with group + 7k at goal race pace = in 30'	Option 2: TIME TRIAL UP HILL*: Palomar mountain twice.

SUNDAY	
RUN: Nice and easy 1h45' Intensity: Easy	TOTAL: 10:45h.

NOTES:
1.- Follow the training as it is.
2.- For the next weekend you have two options. 1frst. Option would be ride with the regular group and right after run 7k at race pace = 30' . 2nd option would be to do a time trial up to Palomar mountain twice. There is this group of cyclist Marci is training (8 cyclist) that are going to do it. And it could be very fun and good for you. I am going to participate.

WEEK NUM. 6 FROM MARCH 1 TO 7 2.004
(last phase: specific workouts)

MONDAY	
SPINNING: 2 hours spinning back to back. Intensity: Easy. Use this session to recover from the weekend.	

TUESDAY	
WEIGHTS: Weights for legs.+ 1 mile on the treadmill fast!.	**TRACK:** (Specific workout for California) 3 x (400m in 1'30"+ 600m in 2'15"+ 1.000m in 3'47") all with 100m walk in between.

WEDNESDAY	
MASTERS' SWIM: Whatever they ask you. Intensity: Easy (H.R Max 162b.p.m)	**RUNNING:** 1h.15' Nice and easy run. Intensity: Low, up to 153bpm

THURSDAY	
RUNNING: 1h. Easy run Intensity: Moderate, up to 162bpm.	**BIKING:** (on the road or on the turbo training) 2h with specific bike workout 3. S.B.W 3: W.U + 6 x (1'R. Leg + 1' L.Leg + 2' really hard, up to 175bpm.) + 10' nice and easy + 6' at race pace (170bpm) + Cool down

FRIDAY	
MASTERS' SWIM: At least 4.000yards. Whatever they ask you. With a test of 1.500y in 20' Intensity: Moderate	

SATURDAY	
SATURDAY WORKOUT = 6h45' 6h biking (153 bpm) + 10k in 45'	

SUNDAY	
RUNNING: 1h and 45' nice and easy	TOTAL: 18:45'.

NOTES:
1.- Long week!
2.- For last weeks, as important as training is resting. If you have a day where you feel too tired to workout, don't do it! rest and let your body get ready for the following day.
3.- Weight workouts: 3 sets of 12,10,8 repts per each exercise with longer rest in between and much more weight. You are looking for power.
4.- No more endurance-strenght weight training.
5.- Friday workout: Look for someone who can pace you for part of the test.

WEEK NUM. 7 FROM MARCH 8 TO 14
2.004 (last phase: specific workouts)

MONDAY	
SPINNING:1h. Intensity: Moderate.	SWIMMING: 1h. Intensity: Moderate up to high.
TUESDAY	
SPINNING:2h. option2 (and the best) BIKING: 2h. Intensity: Moderate. Up to 162bpm.	TRACK: (Specific workout for California) 6 x 1000m in 3'47". 400m rest in between.
WEDNESDAY	
MASTERS' SWIM: Whatever they ask you. (but from now on 90% of the workout needs to be freestyle) Intensity: Easy (H.R Max 162b.p.m)	RUNNING: OFF
THURSDAY	
RUNNING: 1h. Easy run Intensity: Moderate, up to 162bpm.	BIKING: (on the road or on the turbo training) 1h20' with specific bike workout 4. S.B.W 4: W.U + 9' (45"'R. Leg + 45" L.Leg) + 10' nice and easy 1' (53 x16) gear 1' (53 x15) + 3 x 1' (53x14) 1' (53x13) 1' (53x13) standing up + Cool down
FRIDAY	
OFF	
SATURDAY	
SATURDAY WORKOUT 3h maximum with Saturday ride + 3k really nice and easy.	
SUNDAY	
TEMECULA SPRINT TRIATHLON.	TOTAL: UP TO 13:20'.

NOTES:
1.- Tuesday. You have two options, best would be the second one.
2.- Saturday. Still training, but take it easy really easy.
3.- Sunday. First real test. You won't be totally rested, almost better I
    don't want your time to put pressure on you for the ½ Ironman.
4.- Good practice to know better what to do during the transitions,
    and get more efficient on them.

WEEK NUM. 8 FROM MARCH 15 TO 21
2.004 (last phase: specific workouts)

MONDAY	
SPINNING+SPINNING: 1h +1h.	
Intensity: Moderate	Intensity: Moderate up to high

TUESDAY	
WEIGHTS: Weights for legs.+ 1 mile on the treadmill fast!. Weights: 5 sets = 12,10,10,8,8 reps. per each exercise.	TRACK: (Specific workout for California) 4 x 1.600m in 5'48". 400m rest in between.

WEDNESDAY	
MASTERS' SWIM: Whatever they ask you. (but from now on 90% of the workout needs to be freestyle) Intensity: Easy (H.R Max 162b.p.m)	RUNNING: 1h30' nice and easy, up to 153bpm.

THURSDAY	
RUNNING: 1h. Easy run Intensity: Easy, up to 153bpm.	BIKING: (on the road or on the turbo training) 1h20' with specific bike workout 5 (power). S.B.W 5: W.U + 10' (20"'R. Leg + 20" L.Leg) Longest gear you have. + 20' (30"sprint + 1'30" easy) Longest gear you have. + Cool down

FRIDAY	
SWIMMING: Whatever they ask you, swim as long as possible. Perfect goal 4.000 Intensity: Moderate.	

SATURDAY	
SATURDAY WORKOUT 3h maximum with Saturday ride group, easy pace+ 5k moderate.	

SUNDAY	
"RIDE 4 AIDS BIKE RIDE" 50miles	TOTAL: UP TO 16:20'.

NOTES:

1.- This is your last long week. After this, all is down hill. Now, you have to listen your body more than ever, so if you feel tired just skip the workout and rest. Actualy the "home work" is done.

2.- Tuesday. Weights: Power!! You want to rest 1'30" at least after each set, and lift as much weight as possible. If you don't want to rest so long, you can go from one exercise to another of a compleatly different mucular group, without almos any rest. Exem. One set of squats and then one set for calf. It is hard to give 100% in each set though.

3.- Sunday. First real test. As I told you, you need to compete in order to get use to compete, the more you compete the better you do it. So on Sunday give your best!

WEEK NUM. 9 FROM MARCH 22 TO 28 2.004 (tapering)

MONDAY
OFF

TUESDAY
TRACK: (Specific workout for California) 6 x 1.000m in 3'47". 400m rest in between.

WEDNESDAY	
MASTERS' SWIM: Whatever they ask you. (but from now on 90% of the workout needs to be freestyle) Intensity: Easy (H.R Max 155b.p.m)	RUNNING: OFF.

THURSDAY	

Option 1: SPINNING:
Sinning with Carles at 6:00pm
Intensity: High
	Option 2: BIKING: (on the road!)
	1h20' with specific bike workout 6 (race
	  pace simulation).
	S.B.W 6: W.U
	  + 3 x 10' really hard.
	  + 7' rest in between.
	  + Cool down

FRIDAY
OFF

SATURDAY
SATURDAY WORKOUT: 2:30' bike ride at unconfortable pace from the beginning to the end. + 20' easy run.

SUNDAY	
MINI-TRIATHLON: 30' swimming + 44'.biking + 40' running .	TOTAL: UP TO 8:00

NOTES:

1.- WE MADE IT!! As you can see this is the firsrt one of the two tapering weeks. Is really important that you don't do more than what it says in the schedule. We went a long way get to the tapering weeks, the work is done, now is time to rest, and be ready!

2.- Thursday. You have 2 options, in case you can't do option 2, come to my the spinning class.

3.- Here we go again: Sunday. This is going to be your personal test. Look for somone that wants to do it with you (may be Fred, since he is training for wildflowers), or just go by yourself. But either way you need to go as fast as possible.
Here are the times you should to achieve:
  30' swim = 200 warm up + 2000 yards in 27'
  + 5' transition. You can't take longer than that to be cycling on your bike.
  + Bike length: From the club to where the Saturday ride meets. You will take San Dieguito road by fairbanks ranch. One way and back = 44'

WEEK NUM. 10 FROM MARCH 29 TO 4 2.004 (tapering)

MONDAY	
OFF	
TUESDAY	
TRACK: (Specific workout for California) 2 x 1.600m in 5'45". 400m rest in between.	
WEDNESDAY	
MASTERS' SWIM: Only 45'!!! Whatever they ask you. (but from now on 90% of the workout needs to be freestyle) Intensity: Easy (H.R Max 155b.p.m)	RUNNING: OFF.
THURSDAY	
OFF	
FRIDAY	
35' easy biking + 30' nice and easy run	
SATURDAY	
CALIFORNIA 1/2 IRONMAN Total time: 5h.8'51" (27'58" + 2h.48'59" + 1h44'49")	
SUNDAY	
OFF	TOTAL: UP TO 2:45' + RACE

NOTES:
1.- There is nothing else to do but resting.
2.- Thursday. The biking must be done with your race bike.

11 WEEKS TRAINING FOR A 6:30 TO 7 HOURS HALF IRONMAN

Athlete: Angela Lau (Female)
Age: 47
Weight: 120lbs
Status: Single
Profession: Journalist
Base training prior to the program: 10h to 13h. a week
Time available for training: 18 hours a week the most
Her best sport: Running
Groups: Master swimming at UCSD , Organize turbo training with Terry Martin group.
Goal for the seasson: Finish her first ½ Ironman

WEEK NUM. 1 FROM JANUARY 3 TO 9 2.005:

MONDAY
OFF

TUESDAY
BIKE: Specific training (S.T) 1 W.U 20' nice and easy + 5 x (1' left leg + 1' right leg) + 5 x (1' tempo ride + 1' Sprint + 3' recovering, easy and short gear) + 30' nice and easy 1h 45' Total.

WEDNESDAY	
MASTERS' SWIM: 1h swim. Intensity: Really easy.	TURBO TRAINING: This week yes! Whatever they ask you. Intensity: Moderate up to 85%

THURSDAY
WEIGHTS + SPINING: Weights routine 3 + Spinning 1h. Intensity: High.

FRIDAY
MASTERS' SWIM: 1h swim. Intensity: Moderate

SATURDAY
BRICK BIKE TO RUN: 2h +15'. Really nice and easy. You can choose any roat. Right after 15' nice and easy run

SUNDAY	
RUNNING:1h30' Your long run of the week. 1h.30' Nice and easy run.	TOTAL TIME:12:00'

NOTES:
1.-This week is long, be careful. Also is the first week as a training for ½ IM California.
2.- Sunday your long run like always. You will build that up to 2h.

WEEK NUM. 2 FROM JANUARY 10 TO 16 2.005:

MONDAY
OFF

TUESDAY
BIKE:2h Specific training (S.T) 2 S.W 2 = ACCELERATIONS w.u nice and easy for 1h then follow the next intervals: (On a flat road) Useing only the longest/hardest gere you have, you need to accelerate from 6 mls/hour up to 20 mls/hour as fast as possible, then change gere and slow down for 4'. Repeat the exercise 6 times. Ride on a flat road. Cool down to home

WEDNESDAY	
RUNNING: 1h easy run (140bpm max)	MASTERS' SWIM: 1h swim. Intensity: Really easy.

THURSDAY
WEIGHTS + RUNNING: Follow the weights workout "routine 1". Repeat the whole workout 3 times. Right after 40' runing nice and easy (140bpm max) Intensity: High.

FRIDAY
MASTERS' SWIM: 1h 15'swim. Intensity: Moderate

SATURDAY
BRICK BIKE TO RUN: 2h 15'+25'. Really nice and easy. You can choose any road. Right after 25' nice and easy run

SUNDAY	
RUNNING:1h35' Your long run of the week. 1h.35' Nice and easy run (never over 140bpm).	TOTAL TIME:10:45'

NOTES:
1.-This week is your secon week of the micro-cycle
2.-Friday: Swim 15' by yourself before masters.
3.- This time I tell you also, the intensity by b.p.m.

WEEK NUM. 3 FROM JANUARY 17 TO 23 2.005:

MONDAY
OFF

TUESDAY
BIKE: 2h.30 S.T 3 = HILLS 6 x TORREY PINES OUTSIDE ROAD. 1frst. Tempo climb. Always same pace (up to 170bpm) 2nd. Slow climb long gear. The longest/hardest gear you can ride for the entired climb. (160bpm) 3rd. Spinning climb. Shortest gear fast cadence. (150bpm) 4th. Tempo climb again. 5th. One leg climb. ½ of the climb w/right leg, ½ w/left leg. 6th. Accelerations. 1' easy 20" fast al the way to the top. 15' Cool Down Cool down to home

WEDNESDAY	
SWIMMING: 2.000y 2.000 yards nice and easy swim.	RUNNING: 1h easy run (140bpm max)

THURSDAY
WEIGHTS + RUNNING: Follow the weights workout "routine 2". Repeat the whole workout 3 times. Right after 20' runing at 8':00" to 8':10" pace per mile..

FRIDAY
MASTERS' SWIM: 1h 15'swim. Intensity: Moderate

SATURDAY
BIKE + RUN: 3h+20' Nice and easy ride (135bpm max) + right after 20' at 8'to 8'10" /mile

SUNDAY	
RUNNING:1h40' Your long run of the week. 1h.40' Nice and easy run (never over 140bpm).	TOTAL TIME:13:35'

NOTES:
1.-This week is your third week of the micro-cycle, next week you have a active recovering one.
2.- When I tell you to run at 8 to 8:10 mile pace is becouse even it could be hard, this is the pace you should run that workout.I rader preffer you run shorter but at this pace than longer but slower.
3.- We need still to improve your base and endurance, but I think you really are on the right way.

WEEK NUM. 4 FROM JANUARY 24 TO 30 2.005:

MONDAY
OFF
TUESDAY
BIKING: (on the road or on the turbo training) 1h 30' with specific bike workout . S.T 4: 10' (30" pedaling only r.leg +30" l. leg) + 1' hard + 1' easy + 2' hard + 1'easy + 3' hard + 1'easy +2' hard +1' easy + 1'hard + 1'easy + Cool down Hard= up to 90%
WEDNESDAY
MASTERS' SWIM: 1.500y Whatever they ask you. No more than 1.500y. Intensity: Easy(H.R Max 70%)
THURSDAY
OFF
FRIDAY
TRI-TRAINING: Whatever they asck you. Time to give your best.
SATURDAY
SATURDAY WORKOUT = 2h 45'hours 2h biking (153 bpm) + 2.5miles in 23' + cool down.
SUNDAY

RUNNING + STRETCHING: 1h easy run + 1h stretching Intensity : Everything low (HR Max 70%)	TOTAL: 15:50h.

NOTES:

1.- As you can see this is your active recovering week. You did a awesome job last 3 week so now is time for your body to recover and get stronger. So don't do more that what I ask you.

2.- Friday: rest! Doesn't matter if you feel tired or not, rest.

3.- Saturday: Short and easy ride, and right after we will run 2.5 miles in 23' (goal pace for the race)

WEEK NUM. 5 FROM JANUARY 31 TO 6 2.005:

MONDAY
OFF

TUESDAY
BIKING: 2h with specific bike workout . S.T 5: On a flat road or always climbing with the longest/hardest gear you can move. 12' (2'R leg + 2'L.leg) 8' (1'R leg + 1'L.leg) 5' (30"R leg + 30"L.leg) 3' (15"R leg + 15"L.leg) Cool down till the 2h

WEDNESDAY	
MASTERS' SWIM: 2.500 Whatever they ask you. Intensity: Easy(H.R Max 70%)	RUNNING: 1h. Easy run Intensity: Easy, up to 70% to 75%

THURSDAY	
BIKING: 2h Nice and easy biking. Intensity: Easy, up to 70% to 75%	RUNNING: 40'. Easy run Intensity: Easy, up to 70% to 75%

FRIDAY
RUNNING: 1h. Easy run Intensity: Easy, up to 70% to 75%

SATURDAY
SATURDAY WORKOUT = 3h 40'hours 3h biking (153 bpm) + 3miles in 32' + cool down.

SUNDAY	
RUNNING + STRETCHING: 1h 20'easy run + 1h stretching Intensity : Everything low (HR Max 70%)	TOTAL: 13h40.

NOTES:
1.- First week of volume of the second micro-cycle. Since you are in Idyllwild Thursday, Friday, Saturday and Sunday is going to be all about biking and running. Monday rest, by the way.
2.- Don't worry if this week I don't ask you to swim that much. You will swim next week.

WEEK NUM. 6 FROM FABRUARY 7 TO 13 2.005:

MONDAY	
OFF	
TUESDAY	
BIKING: 2h. Nice and easy ride up to 135bpm	TRACK: (Specific workout for California) 2 x (400m in 1'45"+ 600m in 2'30"+ 1.000m in 4'05") all with 100m walk in between.
WEDNESDAY	
MASTERS' SWIM: 3.000y Whatever they ask you. No more than 3.000y. Intensity: Easy(H.R Max 70%)	WEIGHTS + RUNNING: Follow the weights workout "routine 2". Repeat the whole workout 3 times. Right after 20' runing nice and easy.
THURSDAY	
BIKING: 2h Nice and easy biking. (135bpm max) with S.T 6: 6 x (1'R. Leg + 1' L.Leg + 2' really hard, up to 175bpm.) + 10' nice and easy + 6' at race pace (170bpm) Cool down till you ride the 2h.	
FRIDAY	
MASTERS' SWIM: 3.000y Whatever they ask you. No more than 3.000y. Intensity: Easy(H.R Max 70%)	RUNNING: 45'. Easy run Intensity: Easy, up to 70% to 75%
SATURDAY	
SATURDAY WORKOUT = 3hours + run 3h biking (153 bpm Max) + 2 miles nice and easy	
SUNDAY	
SANDIEGUITO ½ MARATHON:	TOTAL: 12h5' + Race.

NOTES:
1.- Second week of volume of the second micro-cycle. It is your first week with track workout, so be careful. The time are only orientative, so if you feel that you are going way too hard just slow down and do your best that day, but don't get injured!!
2.- Sunday: I would like you run the San Dieguito ½ marathon, unfortunatly is going to be at the end of a long training week, therefore your time is not going to be fast, but I just want you race to get the feeling of racing.

WEEK NUM. 7 FROM FABRUARY 14 TO 20 2.005:

MONDAY	
OFF	
TUESDAY	
BIKING:	
WEDNESDAY	
MASTERS' SWIM: 3.000y Whatever they ask you. No more than 3.000y. Intensity: Easy(H.R Max 70%)	
THURSDAY	
BIKING: 2h Nice and easy biking. (145bpm max)	TRACK: (Specific workout for California) 6 x 1000m in 4'15" to 4'20". 400m rest in between.
FRIDAY	
MASTERS' SWIM: 2.000y Whatever they ask you. No more than 2.000y. Intensity: Easy(H.R Max 70%)	
SATURDAY	
SATURDAY WORKOUT = 4hours + run 4h biking (153 bpm Max) + 3 miles in 24'	
SUNDAY	
SWIMMING +RUNNING: 1h 10'+ 1h45' 2.500y, nice and easy (not longer than 1h10') Nice and easy run up to 140bpm max.	TOTAL: 14h45'

> NOTES:
> 1.-Third week of volume of the second micro-cycle. After this a rest
>   week, and then the rest is all down hill til the race. Come on last
>   pull!! ☺
> 2.- Try to follow the schedule as close as possible

WEEK NUM. 8 FROM FEBRUARY 21 TO 27 2.005:

MONDAY	
OFF	
TUESDAY	
BIKING: (on the road or on the turbo training) 2h. with specific bike workout (power). S.T 8: W.U + 10' (20'''R. Leg + 20'' L.Leg) Longest gear you have. + 20' (30''sprint + 1'30'' easy) Longest gear you have. + Cool down	TRACK: (Specific workout for California) 4 x 1.600m in 6'20''. 400m rest in between.
WEDNESDAY	
MASTERS' SWIM: 2.500y Whatever they ask you. No more than 2.500y. Intensity: Easy(H.R Max 70%)	
THURSDAY	
OFF	
FRIDAY	
MASTERS' SWIM: 2.000y Whatever they ask you. No more than 2.000y. Intensity: Easy(H.R Max 70%)	RUNNING: 45' 45' really nice and easy
SATURDAY	
SATURDAY WORKOUT = 2hours + run 2h biking (153 bpm Max) + 5 miles in 40'	
SUNDAY	
SWIMMING +RUNNING: 45'h + 1h20' 2.500y, nice and easy (not longer than 45') Nice and easy run up to 140bpm max.	TOTAL: 12h45'

NOTES:
1.- Rest week. Remember that the goal of this week is to recover and therfore to get stronger, so don't do more that what the schedule says.

WEEK NUM. 9 FROM FEBRUARY 28 TO 6 2.005:

MONDAY	
OFF	
TUESDAY	
BIKING: (on the road or on the turbo training) 2h. with specific bike workout (Endurance). S.T 9 W.U + 10' (20"'R. Leg + 20" L.Leg) Longest gear you have. + 20' (30"sprint + 1'30" easy) Longest gear you have. + Cool down	
WEDNESDAY	
MASTERS' SWIM: 2.500y Whatever they ask you. No more than 2.500y. Intensity: Easy(H.R Max 70%)	RUNNING: 45' 45' really nice and easy
THURSDAY	
OFF	
FRIDAY	
MASTERS' SWIM: 2.000y Whatever they ask you. No more than 2.000y. Intensity: Easy(H.R Max 70%)	RUNNING: 45' 45' really nice and easy
SATURDAY	
SATURDAY WORKOUT = 3hours 30' + run *Race simulation	
SUNDAY	
RUNNING: 1h15' Nice and easy run up to 140bpm max.	TOTAL: 10h45'

NOTES:
1.- Well, the work is done, from now on is all down hill. So first most important thing is to be as rested as possible, it is more important be healthy and rested than the workouts, so if by an reasson you feel tired, that's ok just take that day off. As I said the work is done.
2.- Saturday. I am organizing a race simulation. We will leave from my home with some others athletes and we will do an individual time trial (don't worry it will be all different levels), after we will go for a run.

WEEK NUM. 10 FROM MARCH 7 TO
13 2.005 (last phase: tapering)

MONDAY	
OFF	
TUESDAY	
BIKING: (on the road or on the turbo training) 2h. Really easy and mellow pace	
WEDNESDAY	
MASTERS' SWIM: 2.500y Whatever they ask you. No more than 2.500y. Intensity: Easy(H.R Max 70%)	
THURSDAY	
OFF	
FRIDAY	
RUNNING: 45' 45' really nice and easy	
SATURDAY	
SATURDAY WORKOUT Mini-Trathlon = 1h 20'	
SUNDAY	
SWIMMING +RUNNING: 1h10' 1.500y Nice and easy swim + 35' Nice and easy run up to 140bpm max.	TOTAL: 6h15'

NOTES:
1.- The entired week is mellow and easy, please take it this way. The job is done, and there is nothing else but rest that you can do.
2.-Saturday. It is going to be last really hard but short workout. We will do all together a mini-triathlon at PAC. I will call you and let you know.

WEEK NUM. 11 FROM MARCH 14 TO 20 2.005:

MONDAY	
OFF	
TUESDAY	
OFF	YOGA: Whatever they ask you
WEDNESDAY	
BIKING: 1h 30' 1h Nice and easy biking Intensity: Low up to 145bpm	
THURSDAY	
OFF	
FRIDAY	
SWIM + RUNNING: 20'+ 30'.	
SATURDAY	
½ IRONMAN CALIFORNIA: Total Time: 6h.38'	
SUNDAY	
OFF	TOTAL TIME: 2:20'+ 1h Yoga + Race

NOTES:

1.- It is time to rest as much as possible. Again the work is done, and I think you are more ready than ever.

2.- Race day = All out!!!

3.- You have enough experience to know how much you need to eat or to drink. Advise though is for the warm up. Warm up: 1hour before your start, run for 10' nice and easy + 10' resting and preparing your stuff + 7' running easy + 10' resting and preparing your stuff + 5' nice and easy run + 10' to get at the starting line.

Olympic distance

12 WEEKS TRAINING FOR A SUB.2h. OLYMPIC DISTANCE TRIATHLON:

Athlete: Jessica Lopez (Female)
Age: 28
Weight: 120lbs
Profesion: Pro. Triathlete and duathlete.
Ranck #1 Duathlete in USA
Base training prior to the program: 20 week
Time available for training: Every day, conditioned by work.
Groups: Master swimming group, cycling group.
Goal for the seasson: Triathlon and Duathlon Olympic distance races.

WEEK NUM. 1 FROM FEBRUARY 14 TO 20 2.005:

MONDAY
OFF

TUESDAY
BIKING + RUNNING :
3h. of nice and easy biking (148rpm max). + 1h.15' nice and easy run (140bpm max)

WEDNESDAY	
WEIGHTS + RUNNING:	
Follow the weights workout "routine 1". Repeat the whole workout 3 times. Right after 1h easy run	SWIMMING: 1h45' 5.000m. medium pace.

THURSDAY	
BIKING + RUNNING:	
3h30' nice and easy biking (135bpm max) With: <u>S.T 1</u>: . 9' (45"'R. Leg + 45" L.Leg) + 10' nice and easy 1' (53 x16) gear 1' (53 x15)	+ 3 x 1' (53x14) 1' (53x13) 1' (53x13) standing up + Cool down + 50' nice and easy run (140bpm max)

FRIDAY	
RUNNING: 1h 15' nice and easy run (140bpm max)	SWIMMING: 5.000m. Time to push again, with your swimming group. Intensity: 95% of your max HR effort.

SATURDAY	
BIKING + RUNNING:	
3h30' biking (150bpm max)+ 50' nice and easy run (140bpm max)	

SUNDAY	
RUNNING: 2h 2h nice and easy run (140bpm max)	TOTAL TIME: Up to 20h.45'

NOTES:
1.- First week of volume from the third micro-cycle.
2.- It is really TIME to put in some miles.

WEEK NUM. 2 FROM FEBRUARY 21 TO 27 2.005:

MONDAY
OFF

TUESDAY
BIKING + RUNNING :   3h. of nice and easy biking (148rpm max). + 1h.20' nice and easy run (140bpm max)

WEDNESDAY	
WEIGHTS + RUNNING: Follow the weights workout "routine 2". Repeat the whole workout 3 times. Right after 1h easy run	SWIMMING: 1h45' 5.000m. easy, easy pace. Long sets, anywhere between 300m and 500m.

THURSDAY
BIKING + RUNNING: 3h30' nice and easy biking (135bpm max)   With: S.T 2:   W.U +   10' (20"'R. Leg + 20" L.Leg) Longest gear you have.   + 20' (30"sprint + 1'30" easy) Longest gear you have.   + Cool down.   + 1h nice and easy run (140bpm max)

FRIDAY	
RUNNING: 1h 20' nice and easy run (140bpm max)	SWIMMING: 5.000m. Time to push again, with your swimming group. Intensity: 95% of your max HR effort.

SATURDAY
BIKING + RUNNING: 4h biking (150bpm max)+ 40' nice and easy run (140bpm max)

SUNDAY	
RUNNING: 2h 2h nice and easy run (140bpm max)	TOTAL TIME: Up to 22h.25'

NOTES:
1.- Second week of volume from the third and last volume micro-cycle.
2.- It is really the TIME to put in some miles + it is important you keep your HR low, remember that the goal of this phase is just to increase your body's strenth and endurance, not your times. I know is not fun to go so slow for so long, just 2 more weeks of patience.
3.- Thursday. On those bike 30"sprint you can go as hard as you want.

WEEK NUM. 3 FROM FEBRUARY 28 TO 6 2.005:

MONDAY
OFF

TUESDAY
RUNNING + BIKING: 1h. nice and easy run (140bpm max) + 3h. of nice and easy biking (148rpm max).

WEDNESDAY	
WEIGHTS + RUNNING: Follow the weights workout "routine 3". Repeat the whole workout 3 times. Right after 45' easy run	SWIMMING: 50' 2.500m. <u>Work out 1</u>: W.U 500m + 300m easy with pull and paddles + 4 x 50in 33" + 27" rest + 300 easy pull & paddles + 4 x 50 in 33" + 27" rest + 300m pull& paddles + 8 x 25m in 16" + 30" rest + 500m Cool down

THURSDAY
BIKING + RUNNING: 3h nice and easy biking (135bpm max) + 45' nice and easy run (140bpm max)

FRIDAY
RUNNING: 1h 20' nice and easy run (140bpm max)

SATURDAY
SATURDAY WORKOUT = 3hours 30' + run *Race simulation

SUNDAY	

SWIMMING:
2.500m. Time to push again.
Intensity: 95% of your max HR effort.
<u>Work out 2:</u> W.U 500m easy +
5 x 100m in 1' 10" (recovering 100 really
  easy in between intervals + 100m nice
  and easy between sets)
6 x 50m in 32"
6 x 25" in 15"or less
Cool down 200m
<u>RUNNING:</u> 1h 30'
1h30' nice and easy run (140bpm max)
	TOTAL TIME: Up to 19h.

NOTES:
1.- Third week of volume from the third and last volume micro-cycle.
2.- Saturday. I am organizing a race simulation. We will leave from my home with some others athletes and we will do an individual time trial (don't worry it will be all different levels), after, we will come home and we will go for a run. It is going to be your first test.

WEEK NUM. 4 FROM MARCH 7 TO 13
2.005 (last phase: tapering)

MONDAY
OFF
TUESDAY
BIKING: (on the road or on the turbo training) 2h. Really easy and mellow pace
WEDNESDAY
SWIMMING: 45' Easy swim, just to strecht out your muscles.
THURSDAY
OFF
FRIDAY
RUNNING: 45' 45' really nice and easy
SATURDAY
SATURDAY WORKOUT Mini-Trathlon = 1h 20'
SUNDAY

RUNNING: 1h10' 1h10' really nice and easy run up to 140bpm max.	TOTAL: 7h

NOTES:
1.- The entired week is mellow and easy, please take it this way. The job is done, and there is nothing else but rest that we can do. After this week we start (finally!!) the specific phase.
2.- Saturday. I am going to organize a mini-triathlon at PAC, it will be great if you could come to join us. Is the only really hard workout this week.

WEEK NUM.5 FROM MARCH 14 TO 20
2.005 (Specific training for Alabama)

MONDAY
OFF

TUESDAY
RUNNING + BIKING: 45'. nice and easy run (140bpm max) + S.T 3 30' wu + 2 x 2' (1'easy) 2 x 3' (1'easy) all of them at 22.2miles/h 2 x 4' (1'easy) 2 x 5' + 30' Cool Down

WEDNESDAY	

WEIGHTS + RUNNING:
Follow the weights workout "routine 1".
  Repeat the whole workout 3 times.
Right after 30' easy run
	SWIMMING:
	2.500m. Time to push again.
	Intensity: 95% of your max HR effort.
	Work out 1: W.U 500m easy +
	5 x 100m in 1' 15" (recovering 1full min. in
	  between intervals + 100m nice and easy
	  between sets)
	6 x 75m in 56"
	6 x 50m in 35"
	6 x 25" in 17"or less
	Cool down 300m

THURSDAY
OFF

FRIDAY
BIKING + TRACK: 1h 45' at 20 miles/h average (included w.u) + Track

1 x 1.600m in 5'32" to 5'44"	1 x 400m in 1'16" to 1'19"
1 x 1.200m in 4'03" to 4'14"	1 x 200m in 32" to 36'
1 x 800m in 2:35" to 2'42"	

(rest: as long as you need to make the times)

SATURDAY
BIKING + RUNNING: 2h30 nice and easy biking (135bpm max) + 25' nice and easy run (140bpm max)

SUNDAY	
SWIMMING: 1h45' 5.000m. easy, easy pace. Long sets, anywhere between 300m and 500m. RUNNING: 1h10' 1h10' Tempo pace = 6'25" x mile	TOTAL: 13h15'

NOTES:
1.- Ok, we have to change our philosophy, quality& rest versus quantity. Your training will be mostly at midle-high intensity, so get use to it., therfore they will be shorter and you have an extra day off a week, to make sure you recover properly.
2.- Tuesday: Easy run + Hard biking
3.- Wednesday: Easy cardiobascular day
4.- Friday: Tempo biking + Hard run
5.- Saturday: Your long day, easy and easy.
6.- Sunday: Your tempo run. If you really want to get strong on your run, this is the moment. Don't go any faster or longer thouhg

WEEK NUM.6 FROM MARCH 21 TO 27
2.005 (Specific training for Alabama)

MONDAY
OFF

TUESDAY
RUNNING + BIKING: 45'. nice and easy run (140bpm max) + S.T 4 30' wu + 2 x 4' (3'easy) 2 x 5' (3'easy) all of them at 22.2miles/h 2 x 6' (3'easy) 2 x 7' + 30' Cool Down

WEDNESDAY	
WEIGHTS + RUNNING: Follow the weights workout "routine 2". Repeat the whole workout 3 times. Right after 35' easy run	SWIMMING: 1h. NICE AND EASY!! 3.000m. <u>Work out 4:</u> W.U 500m + + 4 x 500m easy = 5 (75 free+25stroke) 500m Cool down

THURSDAY
OFF

FRIDAY

BIKING + TRACK:
1h 45' at 20 miles/h average (included w.u)
+ Track

1 x 1.600m in 5'32"	1 x 200m in 34"
1 x 200m in 32"	1 x 1.600m in 5'44"
1 x 1.600m in 5'40"	1 x 200m in 36"

(rest: as long as you need to make the times)

SATURDAY
BIKING + RUNNING: 2h30 nice and easy biking (135bpm max) + 25' nice and easy run (140bpm max)

SUNDAY	

SWIMMING + BIKING + RUNNING :
  (Brick 4)
Swimming 300m easy + 10km on the bike
  easy + 2k run in 6'30"!!+ (10'rest in
  between sets)
Swimming 300m in 3'45" + 10km on the
  bike easy + 2k run easy.
Swimming 300m 3'45" + 10km on the bike
  at 36km/h average + 2k run in 6'30"!!
Cool down 10'
	TOTAL: 12h10'

NOTES:
1.- Ok, you have to change your philosophy, quality & rest versus quantity. Your training will be mostly at midle-high intensity, so get use to it., therfore they will be shorter and you have an extra day off a week, to make sure you recover properly.
2.- Tuesday biking: Each time you go for an interval reset your computer and try to get at least 22,2miles/hour average.
3.-Track workouts. See if you can find some one to run with those days (it is better mentaly), may be Katia?

WEEK NUM. 7 FROM MARCH 28 TO 3
2.005 (Specific training for Alabama)

MONDAY
OFF

TUESDAY

RUNNING + BIKING:
45'. nice and easy run (140bpm max) +
S.T 5
W.U +

+ 1 x 7' race pace. 2'rest	+ 3 x 5' 2'rest	+ 5 x 3' 1'rest
+ 2 x 6' 2'rest	+ 4 x 4' 1'rest	+ 6'x 2' 1'rest

+ 30' Cool Down

WEDNESDAY	
WEIGHTS + RUNNING: Follow the weights workout "routine 3". Repeat the whole workout 3 times. Right after 35' easy run	SWIMMING: 1h. NICE AND EASY!! 2.200m. Work out 5: W.U 500m + + 4 x 100m sprint = 5 (30"rest in between) + 500m nice and easy + 4x 50 sprint + 500m Cool down

THURSDAY
OFF

FRIDAY

BIKING + TRACK:
1h 45' at 20 miles/h average (included w.u)
+ Track
15 x 400m in 1'16" 3' rest

In 1'18" 3' rest	In 1'28" 2'30" rest	In 1'38" 2'10" rest
In 1'20" 2'50" rest	In 1'30" 2' 30" rest	In 1'40" 2' rest
In 1'22" 2'50" rest	In 1'32" 2'20" rest	In 1'42" 2' rest
In 1'24" 2'40" rest	In 1'34" 2'20" rest	In 1'44" 1'50" rest
In 1' 26" 2'40" rest	In 1'36" 2' 10" rest	

SATURDAY

BIKING + RUNNING:
3h nice and easy biking (135bpm max)
+ 25' nice and easy run (140bpm max)

SUNDAY	
RUNNING: 1h 1h Tempo pace = 6'25" x mile	SWIMMING: 2000m nice and easy TOTAL: 13h30'

NOTES:
   1.- I need to know if you still feel too tired or sick at the end of the
      week, if so, we will have to take and extra day off.

WEEK NUM. 8 FROM APRIL 4 TO 10 2.005
(Tappering training for Alabama)

MONDAY
OFF
TUESDAY
RUNNING + BIKING: 25'. nice and easy run (140bpm max) + 1h easy, easy biking
WEDNESDAY
OFF
THURSDAY
BIKING + RUN: 1h easy, easy biking + 30' easy, easy run
FRIDAY
OFF
SATURDAY
BIKING + RUNNING: 45' easy, easy biking + 20' run = 5' warm up + 8 x 100m accelerations (no sprints!) + 100m walk in between + 5' cool down
SUNDAY

POWERMAN ALABAMA	TOTAL: 4h + Race

NOTES:
1.- This week is all about resting and be as much ready as possible for the race day, the work is done. So be nice to your body and let it rest.

WEEK NUM. 9 FROM APRIL 11 TO 17 2.005

MONDAY
OFF

TUESDAY
RUNNING + BIKING: 45' nice and easy run (140bpm max) + 2h. of nice and easy biking (148rpm max).

WEDNESDAY	

WEIGHTS + RUNNING:
Follow the weights workout "routine 1".
  Repeat the whole workout 3 times.
Right after 1h easy run
	SWIMMING: 1h.
	2.650m. <u>Work out 5:</u> W.U 500m +
	+ 5 x 100m free in 1'10"/1'9"/1'8"/1'7"/1'6"
	100 nice and easy in between each 100m +
	  30"rest.
	+ 5 x 50m free in 33"/32"/31"/30"/29"
	100 nice and easy in between each 100m +
	  30"rest.
	+ 6 x 25m in 16"/16"/15"/15"/14"/14" (45" rest)
	All of them starting from the wall. No diving.
	300m Cool down

THURSDAY
BIKING + RUNNING: 3h nice and easy biking (135bpm max) + 45' nice and easy run (140bpm max)

FRIDAY	
RUNNING: 1h 20' nice and easy run (140bpm max)	SWIMMING: 1h. Really, really easy swim. don't count laps, and go by feelings.

SATURDAY
SATURDAY WORKOUT = 3hours 30' + track

SUNDAY	
RUNNING: 1h 30' 1h30' nice and easy run (140bpm max)	TOTAL TIME: Up to 17h.

> **NOTES:**
> 1.- This week is a volume week, take it at low intensity except for the
>   track workout on Saturday.

WEEK NUM. 10 FROM APRIL 18 TO 24 2.005

MONDAY
OFF

TUESDAY
RUNNING + BIKING: 45' nice and easy run (140bpm max) + 2h. of nice and easy biking (148rpm max).

WEDNESDAY	

WEIGHTS + RUNNING:
Follow the weights workout "routine 1".
   Repeat the whole workout 3 times.
Right after 1h easy run
	SWIMMING: Race simulation.
	Go to the lake and repeat the following:
	Race start simulation sprinting 50m from
	   the beach + really easy swim back to the
	   beach. +
	" " Sprinting 100m +
	" " Sprinting 150m +
	" " Sprinting 200m +
	" " Sprinting 250m +
	" " Sprinting 200m +
	" " Sprinting 150m +
	" " Sprinting 100m +
	" " Sprinting 50m +
	Cool down

THURSDAY
BIKING + RUNNING: 3h nice and easy biking (135bpm max) + 45' nice and easy run (140bpm max)

FRIDAY
RUNNING: 1h 20' nice and easy run (140bpm max)

SATURDAY
SATURDAY WORKOUT = 3hours 30' + track

SUNDAY	
RUNNING: 1h 30' 1h30' nice and easy run (140bpm max)	SWIMMING: 2000m nice and easy TOTAL TIME: Up to 16h30'.

NOTES:
   1.- This week is a volume week, take it at low intensity except for the
      track workout on Saturday.

WEEK NUM. 11 FROM APRIL 25 TO 1 2.005

MONDAY
OFF

TUESDAY
TRACK + BIKING: W.U 15' + 3 x 1.600m in 5'35" to 5'40" + 2h. of nice and easy biking (148rpm max) right after.

WEDNESDAY

WEIGHTS + RUNNING: Follow the weights workout "routine 2". Repeat the whole workout 3 times. Right after 1h run at 6'35"/mile	SWIMMING: 1h.20' 3.000m. Workout 6: W.U 500m + + 5 x 100m free in 1'10"/1'9"/1'8"/1'7"/1'6" 100 nice and easy in between each 100m + 30"rest. + 5 x 100m free = 4 x (half length moderate/half length sprint) 100 nice and easy in between each 100m + 30"rest. + 10 x 25m = (half length sprint + stop in the midle of the pool +sprint the rest of the length) (45" rest) All of them starting from the wall. No diving. 250m Cool down

THURSDAY
BIKING + RUNNING: 3h nice and easy biking (135bpm max) + 45' run at 6'35"/mile

FRIDAY
OFF	SWIMMING: 1h. Really, really easy swim. don't count laps, and go by feelings.

SATURDAY
SATURDAY WORKOUT = 3hours 30' + run 3h30' ride at 20m/h average + 2 x 2.000m in 7:05, & 7:10. 4' easy jogging in between

SUNDAY
RUNNING: 1h 30' 1h30' nice and easy run (140bpm max)	SWIMMING: 2000m nice and easy TOTAL TIME: Up to 16h.

> NOTES:
> 1.- This is a specific week. You shouldn't have any problem to do the times and the distances. Just remember to eat and rest as much as your busy schedule allows you.

WEEK NUM. 12 FROM MAY 2 TO 8 2.005

MONDAY
OFF
TUESDAY
*DUATHLON: 1h15' Total. + Warm up Intensity: Race pace
WEDNESDAY
OFF
THURSDAY
SWIMMING: 45' 1.750m. Workout 7: W.U 500m + 10 x 100m free. In

1'40"	1'35"	1'30"	1'25"	1'20"

Once you get at 1'20, you repet 1'20" and go up. (times are with rest included)
250m Cool down

FRIDAY
OFF
SATURDAY
RUNNING: 35' Nice and easy run Intensity: low up to 140 bpm. + 5 accelerations of 100yards (if it is possible up hill)

SUNDAY	
TRIATHLON OLIMPIC DISTANCE Total time: 1h55'	TOTAL TIME: Up to 6h.+ Race

NOTES:
1.- Triathlon: Drive to the flat road by golf course close to your
   house. W.u 15' running . Then run 2 miles at race pace= 6'pace
   + get on your bike and ride as hard as you can till the first
   intersection (where we used to turn right to go to Del Dios) and
   back (about 20kms total) + 2 miles negative splits = 6' + <6'. Then
   15' cool down.
2.- Rest of the week easy.

10 WEEKS TRAINING FOR A 2h. TO 2h.30′ OLYMPIC DISTANCE TRIATHLON:

Athlete: Marianne Rutschi (Female)
Age: 32
Weight: 125lbs
Best result in Olympic distance triathlon: 2h.6'
Profesion: Pro. Triathlete in Oylimpic distance since 2002. Third in the Pro Cup Swiss championship.
Base training prior to the program: 20 to 25h a week
Time available for training: Every day and hours
Her best sport: Age 8 – 18 Swimmer in the Swiss Championship
Groups: Cycling team, master swimming group.
Goal for the seasson: Swiss Triathlon series championship

WEEK NUM. 1 FROM MAY 9 TO 15 2.005:

MONDAY	
BIKING: 2h30' Nice and easy ride. Your hard rate should be at 70% of your max HR effort.	RUNNING (track workout): 15' w.u 1 x 1.600 in 6'00" to 6'10" (Rest in between 400m in all of them) 1 x 1.200 in 4'23" to 4'35" 1 x 1.000 in 3'39" to 3'49" 1 x 800 in 2'48" to 2'55" 1 x 400 in 1'22" to 1'25" 1 x 200 in 35" to 40" Cool Down 10'
TUESDAY	
SWIMMING: 1h45' 5.000m. medium pace.	RUNNING: (Steady run) 12km at 4'12"to 4'19"/km
WEDNESDAY	
OFF	BIKING: 2h30' Time to push a litle bit, with your cycling team Intensity: Up to 95% of your max HR effort.
THURSDAY	
OFF	
FRIDAY	
SWIMMING: 5.000m. Time to push again, with your swimming group. Intensity: 95% of your max HR effort.	
SATURDAY	
OFF	
SUNDAY	
SWIMMING + RUNNING: (Brick 1) 500m easy swim + 10' run at 4'12"/km (10'rest in between) 500m in 6'40" + 10' run at 5'/km 500m in 6'40" + 10' run at 4'12"/km Cool down in the water 400m.	TOTAL TIME: 12h.

NOTES:
1.- First Specific workout week.
2.- The most important part is the recovering. I rather prefer you run 2 x400 in 1'25" that 3x400 in 1'35", in other words we want intensity not distance. Therefore, the workouts need to be shorter but faster.
3.- The times may feel easy, but each week we will train closer to your race pace. We just can't start that fast.

WEEK NUM. 2 FROM MAY 16 TO 22 2.005:

MONDAY	
BIKING: 2h30' Nice and easy ride.Your hard rate should be at 70% of your max HR effort.	RUNNING (track workout): 15' w.u 8 X 1 x 100 in 15' to 17". (Rest in between 200m in all of them) 1 x 200 in 33" to 36" Cool Down 10'

TUESDAY	
SWIMMING: 1h45' 5.000m. easy, easy pace. Long sets, anywhere between 300m and 500m.	RUNNING: (Steady run) 10km at 4'10"to 4'15"/km

WEDNESDAY
OFF

THURSDAY

BIKING: 2h15'
Time to push a litle bit. Warm up nice and easy. (135bpm max)+ specific training.
S.T 1: : W.U
10 x (3' race pace+ 1' as fast as possible with the longest gear possible)
+ 4' really easy in between sets.
Cool down till you ride the 2h15'.
Intensity: Up to 95% of your max HR effort.

FRIDAY

SWIMMING:
2.500m. Time to push again.
Intensity: 95% of your max HR effort.
Work out 1: W.U 500m easy +
(recovering 1full min. in between intervals + 100m nice and easy between sets)

5 x 100m in 1' 15"	6 x 75m in 56"	6 x 50m in 35"	6 x 25" in 17"or less

Cool down 300m

SATURDAY
OFF

SUNDAY	
SWIMMING + BIKING: (Brick 2) 500m easy swim + 15km on the bike in 27' (10'rest in between) 500m in 6'35" + 15km on the bike easy 500m in 6'35" + 15km in 26'30" Cool down in the water 400m.	TOTAL TIME: 11h.

NOTES:
1.- Second Specific workout week.
2.- I know it could seem a short week but I really want you try your best to get the times I ask you, and they are every wekk faster and faster.
3.- Sunday workout may seem difficult to organize, but completly necessary.
4.- Monday workout is not a brick. One session in the morning + 1 session in the afternoon.

WEEK NUM. 3 FROM MAY 23 TO 29 2.005:

MONDAY	

BIKING: 2h30'
Nice and easy ride.
Your hard rate should be at 70% of your max
   HR effort.
	RUNNING (track workout):
	W.u 15'
	6 X 1 x 300 in between 49" to 57". (Rest in
	   between 200m in all of them)
	1 x 400 in 1'17" to 1'20"
	Cool Down 10'

TUESDAY
SWIMMING: 50' 2.500m. Work out 2: W.U 500m + 300m easy with pull and paddles + 4 x 50in 33" + 27" rest +   4 x 50 in 33" + 27" rest +   8 x 25m in 16" + 30" rest + 300 easy pull & paddles +   300m pull& paddles +   500m Cool down

WEDNESDAY	
RUNNING: (Steady run) No worm up here! 8 km at 3'50"to 4'00"/km	OFF

THURSDAY
BIKING: 2h30' 2h30' with the bike group Intensity: Up to 98% of your max HR effort.

FRIDAY
OFF

SATURDAY
SWIMMING: 2.500m. Time to push again. Intensity: 95% of your max HR effort. Work out 3: W.U 500m easy + (recovering 100 really easy in between intervals + 100m nice and easy between sets) 5 x 100m in 1' 10"   6 x 50m in 32"   6 x 25" in 15"or less   Cool down 200m

SUNDAY	
RUNNING + BIKING: (Brick 3) 2k run in 6'30" + 10km on the bike easy (10'rest in between sets) 2k run in 8'30" + 10km in 17' 2k run in 7' + 10km on the bike in 17' Cool down 10'	TOTAL TIME: 10h.

NOTES:
1.- Third Specific workout week.
2.- I know it could seem a short week but I really want you try your
   best to get the times I ask you, and they are every week faster and
   faster.
3.- Monday 30th OFF

WEEK NUM. 4 FROM MAY 30 TO 5 2.005:

MONDAY
OFF
TUESDAY
SWIMMING: 1h. NICE AND EASY!! 3.000m. Work out 4: W.U 500m + + 4 x 500m easy = 5 (75 free+25stroke) 500m Cool down
WEDNESDAY
BIKING: 2h30' 2h30' with the bike group Intensity: Up to 98% of your max HR effort.
THURSDAY
OFF
FRIDAY
RUNNING: (Steady run) No warm up here! 10 km at 3'50"to 4'00"/km
SATURDAY
OFF
SUNDAY

SWIMMING + BIKING + RUNNING : (Brick 4)
Swimming 300m easy + 10km on the bike easy + 2k run in
    6'30"!!+ (10'rest in between sets)
Swimming 300m in 3'45" + 10km on the bike easy + 2k run easy.
Swimming 300m 3'45" + 10km on the bike at 36km/h average +
    2k run in 6'30"!!
Cool down 10'
	TOTAL TIME: 6h.15'

NOTES:
1.- First tapering workout week.
2.- I know it is a really short week, oh well! Enjoy your free time ☺
3.- Monday 6th OFF
4.- There is nothing we can do now, to improve your run. We are to close to the race to run longer. All you can do is try to go as fast as possible on your run's workouts.

WEEK NUM. 5 FROM JUNE 6 TO 12 2.005:

MONDAY
OFF
TUESDAY
SWIMMING: 1h. NICE AND EASY!! 2.200m. Work out 5: W.U 500m + + 4 x 100m sprint = 5 (30"rest in between) + 500m nice and easy + 4x 50 sprint + 500m Cool down
WEDNESDAY
RUNNING: 10' w.u + 2 x 1.500m in 5'12" to 5'24" with 600m rest in between. + 10' cool down
THURSDAY
OFF
FRIDAY
MINI-TRIATHLON: 500m swim + 10k biking + 2k running, all of them slow and easy.
SATURDAY
MURTEN TRIATHLON: All out!! Total Sprint distance triathlon: 1h.14' . 11th Over all pro women.
SUNDAY

SWIMMING: 2000m nice and easy	TOTAL TIME: 3h.40' + Race

NOTES:
1.- Race week.
2.- Rest and get ready for Saturday race.
3.- Monday 13th OFF
4.- No biking on Wednesday, you don't need it.
5.- Saturday: You are more than ready, go for it without fears, be clever and don't let people draft from your wheel on the bike.
6.- You are: Swimmer: Strong (I recoment you to draft in the water, though)
7.- Running: Defenetly your weakest, but still fast, although probably there will be other femels as fast as you or more. (don't try to win the race on the running length).

WEEK NUM. 6 FROM JUNE 13 TO 19 2.005:

MONDAY
OFF

TUESDAY	
SWIMMING: 1h. NICE AND EASY!! 2.300m. Work out 6: W.U 500m + + 8 x 50 sprint (1'rest in between) + 4 x 100m sprint + 2 x 200m hard + 1 x 400 as fast as possible + 500m nice and easy + 200m Cool down	RUNNING: 10' w.u + 2 x 2km in 6'59" with 800m rest in between. + 10' cool down

WEDNESDAY
BIKING: 2h.   Really nice and easy ride.

THURSDAY
OFF

FRIDAY
MINI-TRIATHLON: 500m swim + 10k biking + 2k running, all of them slow and easy.

SATURDAY
ZUG TRIATHLON: All out!!

SUNDAY	
SWIMMING: 2000m nice and easy	TOTAL TIME: 7h. + Race

NOTES:
1.- 2nd race week.
2.- Tuesday is a key workout. Don't do the workouts back to back. You really need to focus in make the times on Tuesday's run. Ask somebody faster than you to help you out.
3.- Monday 20th OFF
4.- Biking on Wednesday easy, you are strong enough you just need to improve your up hills, but now is not the moment, next race you told me is flat anyway.
5.- Saturday: No fears, and all out. You will get better competing everyweek, and don't let athletes draft from you on the bike.

WEEK NUM. 7 FROM JUNE 20 TO 26 2.005:

MONDAY	
OFF	
TUESDAY	
OFF	
WEDNESDAY	
SWIMMING: 1h. 2.650m. <u>Work out 5:</u> W.U 500m + + 5 x 100m free in 1'10"/1'9"/1'8"/1'7"/1'6" 100 nice and easy in between each 100m + 30"rest. + 5 x 50m free in 33"/32"/31"/30"/29" 100 nice and easy in between each 100m + 30"rest. + 6 x 25m in 16"/16"/15"/15"/14"/14" (45" rest) All of them starting from the wall. No diving. 300m Cool down	RUNNING: (easy run) 12 km really nice and easy, don't look at your watch, and go by feelings.
THURSDAY	
BIKING: 2h30' 2h30' with specific workout. SW 1: Today's workout: HILLS!! With: 4 repeats up to a 2km steep hill 1st and 3rd in your 14 or 15 cog, seated. 2nd and 4th the same but standing. Use the down hill to recover. Cool Down . (It is a power exercise, you don't want to go fast, your HR needs to be as low as possible) Cool down till 2h30'	SWIMMING: 1h. Really, really easy swim. don't count laps, and go by feelings.
FRIDAY	
RUNNING: (Steady run) No warm up here! 12 km 4'10"/km = 50' + 1km cool down.	
SATURDAY	
BIKING: 2h30' Really, really easy. Try to do some hills mostly.	
SUNDAY	
SWIMMING + BIKING + RUNNING : (Brick 5) Swimming 300m easy + 10km on the bike easy + 2k run in 8'+ (10'rest in between sets) Swimming 300m in 3'45" + 10km on the bike easy + 2k run easy. Swimming 300m 3'45" + 10km on the bike at 36km/h average + 2k run in 8' Cool down 10'	TOTAL TIME: 10h.30'

NOTES:
1.- Swimming on wednwsday. This is how fast your times need to be in order to be competitive in the water. Rest as much as you need and try no matter what to make the times. Ask someone to help you out.
2.- Bike workout. It is not a speed workout, but a power workout, so you want slow cadence at low HR, but lots of power moving those crancks.
3.-Friday run. Ask some one to pace you.

Carlos Civit

WEEK NUM. 8 FROM JUNE 27 TO 3 2.005:

MONDAY
OFF

TUESDAY

SWIMMING: Race simulation.
Go to the lake and repeat the following:
Race start simulation sprinting 50m from the beach + really easy swim back to the beach. +
 	
  " " Sprinting 100m +   " " Sprinting 200m +
  " " Sprinting 150m +   " " Sprinting 150m +
  " " Sprinting 200m +   " " Sprinting 100m +
  " " Sprinting 250m +   " " Sprinting 50m +
Cool down

WEDNESDAY
RUNNING: 10' w.u + 3 x 1.000m in 3'15" to 3'22" with 600m rest in between. + 10' cool down

THURSDAY
OFF

FRIDAY
MINI-TRIATHLON: 500m swim + 10k biking + 2k running, all of them slow and easy.

SATURDAY
TRIATHLON: All out!!

SUNDAY	
SWIMMING: 2000m nice and easy	TOTAL TIME: 3h.45' + Race

NOTES:
1.- Race week.
2.- Swim workout: Go to a beach by the lake, and simulate race starts, each one longer.
3.- Monday 4th OFF
4.- No biking on Wednesday, you don't need it.
5.- Your swim is stronger than ever!
6.- Warm up: This is what I use to do for warming up. During the 1h prior to the race start, I run 10 minutes nice and easy, and then I stop for 10' more, then I prepare my stuff. Then I run for 10 more minutes and rest again 10', and so on, so on till the start time. I never warm up swimming, it is NOT intens enough, and since ou get wet, it is difficult swim and res, swim and rest.

WEEK NUM. 9 FROM JULY 4 TO 10 2.005:

MONDAY	
OFF	
TUESDAY	
OFF	
WEDNESDAY	

SWIMMING: 1h.20'
 3.000m. <u>Workout 6:</u> W.U 500m +
 + 5 x 100m free in 1'10"/1'9"/1'8"/1'7"/1'6"
 100 nice and easy in between each 100m + 30"rest.
 + 5 x 100m free = 4 x (half length moderate/half
    length sprint)
 100 nice and easy in between each 100m + 30"rest.
 + 10 x 25m = (half length sprint + stop in the middle of
    the pool +sprint the rest of the length) (45" rest)
 All of them starting from the wall. No diving.
 250m Cool down
	RUNNING: (easy run)
	 21 km really nice and easy, don't look at
	   your watch, and go by feelings.

THURSDAY	

BIKING: 3h30'
 3h30' with specific workout.
 <u>SW 2:</u>
 Today's workout: HILLS!!
 With: 10 repeats up to a 2km steep hill
 1st, 3rd, 7th, 9th tempo = at 85% of your max HR.
 in your 21 or 23 cog, seated.
 2nd and 4th and 6th = progressive. You star slow and
    every 200m
 5th and 8th easy recovering climb.you go faster till
    the last 10th is max effort.
 All of them need tobe done with the 21 or 23 cog no
    bigger!!
 Use the down hill to recover.
 Cool Down_.
 Cool down till 3h30'
	SWIMMING: 1h.
	 Really, really easy swim. don't count laps,
	   and go by feelings.

FRIDAY	
RUNNING: (Specific workout)24km. 11kms at nice and easy pace (don't look at the watch + 12 km 4'10"/km = 50' + 1km cool down.	
SATURDAY	

BIKING: 3h30'
 Really, really easy. Try to do some hills mostly.
	RUNNING:
	 10kms nice and easy with 10 x 150m
	   moderate sprint at the end, with 1' rest
	   in between.

SUNDAY	

SWIMMING + BIKING: (Brick 6) (MORNING)
 Swimming 300m at 85% of your max + 10km on the
   bike easy
 (5'rest in between sets)
 Swimming 300m at 90% + 10km on the bike medium
   pace
 Swimming 300m at 98% + 10km on the bike at 36km/h
   average
 Cool down 10'
	BIKING + RUNNING: (Brick 7)
	   (AFTERNOON)
	 10km on the bike easy + 2kms in 9'
	 10km on the bike easy + 2kms in 8'30"
	 10km on the bike easy + 2kms in 8'
	 (3'rest in between sets)
	
	 TOTAL TIME: 15h.50'

NOTES:
Follow the training exacly the way it is. Try to have always a partner
   training with you. Try to make the times even if you feel tired
   that day.

WEEK NUM. 10 FROM JULY 11 TO 17 2.005:

MONDAY
OFF

TUESDAY	

SWIMMING: 45'
1.750m. Workout 7: W.U 500m +
10 x 100m free.
In 1'40"
 	
1'35"   1'30"   1'25"   1'20"
Once you get at 1'20, you repet 1'20" and go up. (times
  are with rest included)
250m Cool down
	RUNNING: (easy run)
	12 km really nice and easy,
	  don't look at your watch,
	  and go by feelings.

WEDNESDAY
BIKING: 2h30' 2h30' with specific workout. SW 3: Today's workout: HILLS!! With: 10 repeats up to a 1km steep hill 1st, 3rd, 7th, 9th tempo = at 85% of your max HR. in your 21 or 23 cog, seated. 2nd and 4th and 6th = progressive. You star slow and every 200m 5th and 8th easy recovering climb.you go faster till the last 10th is max effort. All of them need tobe done with the 21 or 23 cog no bigger!! Use the down hill to recover. Cool down till 2h30'

THURSDAY
SWIMMING: 1h. 2000m. Really nice and easy. Don't look at your watch.

FRIDAY
BIKING + RUNNING: 45' Easy biking + 20' easy running.

SATURDAY		
Zurich Olympic distance triathlon: Total time: 2h.21'.10" (7th Over all pro)		
Swim: 23.08	Bike: 1:12	Run: 45.31

SUNDAY	
BIKING: 2h30' Really nice and easy ride.	TOTAL TIME: 8h.50' + Race

NOTES:
1.- Follow the training exacly the way it is.
2.- Thursday's hill repeats are ½ long than last week. But mostly dont' go
    all out. +-90% to Max effort.
3.- It is a easy week in terms of training, but I think it is the best for you
    now, if you really want to performance on Saturday
4.- Remember it is extremetly difficult and hard course, so times will be slow.

11 WEEKS TRAINING FOR JUST TO FINISH OLYMPIC DISTANCE TRIATHLON:

Athlete: Angela Lau (Female)

Age: 47

Weight: 120lbs

Status: Single

Profession: Journalist

Base training prior to the program: 10h to 13h. a week

Time available for training: 18 hours a week the most

His best sport: Running

Groups: Master swimming at UCSD , Organize turbo training with Terry Martin group.

Goal for the seasson: Triathlons for fun.

WEEK NUM. 1 FROM APRIL 25 TO 1 2.005:

MONDAY
OFF

TUESDAY	
BIKING: 2h30' Nice and easy biking. (140bpm max)	RUNNING: 1h.Nice and easy run = 10'30"miles Intensity: Low up to 145bpm

WEDNESDAY
MASTER SWIMMING: 3.500yards Intensity: high

THURSDAY
BIKING: 1h30' with specific bike workout S.T 1 CLIMBING: W.U + 1 mile at 85% +   10' at 60% +   2 miles at 90% +   5' at 60% +   3 miles at 90% + + Cool down till 1h30'.

FRIDAY	
MASTER SWIMMING: 3.500yards Intensity: low	RUNNING: 45'Nice and easy run = 10'30"miles Intensity: Low up to 145bpm

SATURDAY
BRICK BIKE TO RUN: 2h 45'+ 40'Run. 2h45' nice and easy ride + specific workout on track 4 x 200m in 45" (rest 200m in between) 4 x 400m in 1'50" + 5'Cool down

SUNDAY	
RUNNING: 1h.35' 1h. 30' Nice and easy run.= 10'30" to 11'/ mile (it depends how tired you are) Intensity: Low up to 145bpm	TOTAL TIME: 12:00'

NOTES:
1.- First week of volume .
2.- No weights training yet, see if is possible next week. It would
   depend of your feed backs.

WEEK NUM. 2 FROM MAY 2 TO 8 2.005:

MONDAY	
OFF	
TUESDAY	
BIKING: 2h Nice and easy biking. (140bpm max)	RUNNING: 45'.Nice and easy run = 10'30"miles Intensity: Low up to 140bpm
WEDNESDAY	
MASTER SWIMMING: 3.500yards Intensity: high	
THURSDAY	

BIKING: 2h
2h with specific bike workout
S.T 2 : W.U +
  During 1h, all the up hills will be out of the
  saddle and at 95% intensity, down hills
  and flats will be or recovering or at nice
  and easy pace.
+ Cool down till 1h30'.
	RUNNING:
	45'.Nice and easy run = 10'30"miles
	Intensity: Low up to 140bpm

FRIDAY	
MASTER SWIMMING: 3.500yards Intensity: low	WEIGHTS + RUNNING: Weights: You need to follow the exercises of the routine 3. Execute 15 repetitions per exercise and switcht to the next exercise, and repeat the routine 3 times. Really short rest between exercises. This time, once you finish the 3 times, run 30' at easy/medium pace = 10'00"/ mile.
SATURDAY	
BRICK BIKE TO RUN: 3h + 25'Run. 3h nice and easy ride + specific workout on track 2 x 1.600m in 8'45" (rest 800m in between) + 5'Cool down	
SUNDAY	
RUNNING: 1h.40' 1h. 40' Nice and easy run.= 10'30" to 11'/ mile (it depends how tired you are) Intensity: Low up to 145bpm	TOTAL TIME: 13:10'

NOTES:
1.- Second week of volume .
2.- Finally this week you have weights, since is the first time in a long
    time take it easy, I don't want you too sort the next day.

WEEK NUM. 3 FROM MAY 9 TO 15 2.005:

MONDAY	
OFF	
TUESDAY	
BIKING: 2h Nice and easy biking. (140bpm max)	RUNNING: 45'.Nice and easy run = 10'30"miles with 1 x 1mile in 6:30" Intensity: Low up to 140bpm
WEDNESDAY	
MASTER SWIMMING: 3.500yards Intensity: high	
THURSDAY	
BIKING: 2h 2h with specific bike workout S.T 3 : W.U + 5 x (3' race pace+ 1' at low cadence with 90% tension on your bike + 1' as fast as possible with no tension + 5' nice and easy pace and tension) + Cool down till 2h.	RUNNING: 1h.Nice and easy run = 10'30"miles Intensity: Low up to 140bpm
FRIDAY	
MASTER SWIMMING: 3.000yards Intensity: low	WEIGHTS + RUNNING: Weights: You need to follow the exercises of the routine 1. Execute 15 repetitions per exercise and switcht to the next exercise, and repeat the routine 3 times. Really short rest between exercises. This time, once you finish the 3 times, run 10' at easy/medium pace = 10'00"/ mile.
SATURDAY	
BRICK BIKE TO RUN: 3h + 35'Run. 3h nice and easy ride + specific workout on track 4 x 800m in 3'45" (rest 800m in between) + 5'Cool down	
SUNDAY	
RUNNING: 1h.45' 1h. 45' Nice and easy run.= 10'30" to 11'/ mile (it depends how tired you are) Intensity: Low up to 145bpm	TOTAL TIME: 14:20'

NOTES:
1.- Third week of volume. After this, a rest week.
2.- You are doing an awesome job, keep going!!

WEEK NUM. 4 FROM MAY 16 TO 22 2.005:

MONDAY
OFF

TUESDAY
BIKING: 1h30' Nice and easy biking. (140bpm max)

WEDNESDAY
MASTER SWIMMING: 3.500yards Intensity: easy. Since is your easy week, if during the swim master workout you just swim less than 3.500y stay and keep swimming until you swim those 3.500.

THURSDAY
RUNNING: 1h.Nice and easy run = 10'miles Intensity: Low up to 140bpm

FRIDAY
OFF

SATURDAY
BRICK BIKE TO RUN: 2h + 35'Run. 2h nice and easy ride + specific workout on track 1 x 1200m in between 5'20 and 5'30" 1 x 800m in between 3'37" and 3'47" 1 x 400m in between 1'40" and 1'45" 1 x 200m in between 40" and 45" (rest 400m in between) + 5'Cool down

SUNDAY	
SWIMMING: 2.000yards Nice and easy. Try to swim long sets	TOTAL TIME: 7:30'

NOTES:
1.- Rest week, take it this way.
2.- You are doing an awesome job, keep going!!

WEEK NUM. 5 FROM MAY 23 TO 29 2.005:

MONDAY	
OFF	
TUESDAY	
----------------------	-----------------------
WEDNESDAY	
MASTER'S SWIM: 3.500yards Intensity: Low	WEIGHTS + RUNNING: Weights: You need to follow the exercises of the routine 1. Execute 15 repetitions per exercise and switcht to the next exercise, and repeat the routine 1 3 times. Really short rest between exercises. This time, run 45' nice and easy after the weights.
THURSDAY	
BIKING: 2h30' with specific bike workout S.T 4 : W.U + 9' (2' L.leg + 2' R.leg) 5' n&e 3 X 1'hard 1' easy 1' hard 1' easy 5' nice and easy between sets.	RUNNING: 1h.5'Nice and easy run = 10'45miles Intensity: Low up to 145bpm
FRIDAY	
MASTER'S SWIM : 3.000yards Intensity: Low	
SATURDAY	
BRICK BIKE TO RUN: 4h + 1h.Run. 4h nice and easy ride + 1h easy run right after.	
SUNDAY	
SWIM + RUNNING: 50' + 1h45'. 2.000m easy swim + 1h45'. Nice and easy run.= 10' to 10'30"/ mile (it depends how tired you are) Intensity: Low up to 145bpm	TOTAL TIME: 15:5'

NOTES:
1.- First week of volume. Lots of hours, be careful.
2.- Notice that the times on the run are 30"faster, I think you are ready to go a litle bit faster on your base runs.
3.- Saturday, a big day for you. Be careful with the heat!

WEEK NUM. 6 FROM MAY 30 TO 5 2.005:

MONDAY
OFF

TUESDAY
RUNNING: 1h 50'
1h. 50' Easy run at 10'45" pace

WEDNESDAY	
MASTER'S SWIM: 3.500yards Intensity: Low	WEIGHTS + RUNNING: Weights: You need to follow the exercises of the routine2. Execute 15 repetitions per exercise and switcht to the next exercise, and repeat the routine 1 3 times. Really short rest between exercises. This time, you will run a mile at 8'pace right after every sigle circuit of weights = 3 x 1 mile.

THURSDAY	
BIKING:	
2h30' with specific bike workout	
S.T 5 : W.U +	
8' (2' L.leg + 2' R.leg)	5' n&e
2 X 1'hard out of the saddle	3'hard out of the saddle
2' easy seating down	2' easy seating down
2' hard out of the saddle	4' hard out of the saddle
2' easy seating down	2' easy seating down
5' nice and easy between sets.	

FRIDAY
MASTER'S SWIM : 3.000yards
Intensity: Low

SATURDAY
BRICK BIKE TO RUN: 4h + Track.
4h tempo + intervals.
3 x 2000m.in 11'20" to 11'40"
Run 600m nice and easy in between

SUNDAY	
SWIM + RUNNING: 1h. + 1h. 3.500m easy swim + 1h. Nice and easy run.= 10'45" to 11'/mile (it depends how tired you are) Intensity: Low up to 145bpm	TOTAL TIME: 16:30'

NOTES:
1.- First week of volume. Lots of hours, be careful.
2.- From now on your long rides will be on Tuesday in state of Sunday. I think it will make you recover better.
3.- Saturday, a big day for you. Be careful hith the heat!

WEEK NUM. 7 FROM JUNE 13 TO 19 2.005:

MONDAY	
MASTER'S SWIM: 2.500yards Intensity: Low	WEIGHTS + RUNNING: Weights: You need to follow the exercises of the routine3. Execute 15 repetitions per exercise and switcht to the next exercise, and repeat the routine 1 3 times. Really short rest between exercises. This time, you will run 45'nice and easy

TUESDAY
RUNNING: 1h 55' 1h. 55' Easy run at 10'45" pace. Remember this is going to be your long run of the week.

WEDNESDAY
OFF

THURSDAY	
BIKING: 2h30' with specific bike workout on hills. S.T 6 : W.U +	
8' (2' L.leg + 2' R.leg)	5' n&e
2 X 1'hard seating down	3'hard seating down
2' easy seating down	2' easy seating down
2' hard standing up	4' hard out of the saddle
2' easy standing up	2' easy out of the saddle
Nice and easy till 2h30'	

FRIDAY
MASTER'S SWIM : 1h Whatever they ask you. Intensity: Low

SATURDAY	
BRICK BIKE TO RUN: 2h30+ Track. 2h 30nice and easy biking + intervals.	
2 x 800m.in 3:40 to 4:00	2 x 200m in 50 to 53
2 x 400m in 1:45 to 2:03	2 x100m in 24 to 27
Run 400m nice and easy in between.	

SUNDAY	
SWIM + RUNNING: 1h. + 30'. 2.500m easy swim + 30'. Nice and easy run.= 10'45" to 11'/mile (it depends how tired you are) Intensity: Low up to 145bpm	TOTAL TIME: 12:55'

NOTES:

1.- Second week of volume. Lots of hours, be careful.

2.- Changes: Your day off is Wednesday, so It may be a little bit hard for your body to change. Also remember that on Tuesday you have your long runs.

3.- Saturday, sice you are a litle bit sore, this Saturday has less volume, but the track workouts I are harder.

4.- Remember that we are training for short and Olimpic distance, so it is more important for you to get the speed workouts (weights too) done than the slow and long ones.

WEEK NUM. 8 FROM JUNE 20 TO 26 2.005:

MONDAY	
MASTER'S SWIM: 3.500yards Intensity: Low	WEIGHTS + RUNNING: Weights: You need to follow the exercises of the routine1. Execute 15 repetitions per exercise and switcht to the next exercise, and repeat the routine 1 3 times. Really short rest between exercises. This time, run 45' nice and easy after the weights, the first 10' at 9'00"pace

TUESDAY
RUNNING: 2h 2h. Easy run at 10'00" pace. Remember this is going to be your long run of the week.

WEDNESDAY
OFF

THURSDAY
BIKING: 2h00' with specific bike workout Todays workout: Hills!! With 10' (20"L.leg + 20" R.leg) at 65% effort. 5' n&e regular gear. 3 x (3' seated at 90% effort(slow cadence) + 1'30" at 30% , with high cadence) 10'regular pace + 3 x (3' standing at 90% (slow cadence) + 1'30" at 30% , seated and with high cadence) All of this needs to be done going up hill. (exemple: Torry Pines)

FRIDAY
MASTER'S SWIM : 1h30' Whatever they ask you. + 15' swimming by yourself before the session, and 15' after. Intensity: Low

SATURDAY
BRICK BIKE TO RUN: 2h30+ Track. 2h 30nice and easy biking + interval. 2 x 2000m in 9' resting 800m in between.

SUNDAY	
SWIM + RUNNING: 1h.15' + 40'. 3.500m easy swim + 40'. Nice and easy run.= 10'45" to 11'/mile (it depends how tired you are) Intensity: Low up to 145bpm	TOTAL TIME: 13:10'

NOTES:
1.- Third week of volume. Lots of hours, be careful. 2.- Swimming. This week you are going to put more time into your swimming. 3.- Saturday. The track workout is going to be intens and long. Pace yourself, and try to get the times.

WEEK NUM. 9 FROM JUNE 27 TO 3 2.005:

MONDAY	
OFF	
TUESDAY	
RUNNING: 1h 1h. Easy run at 10'00" pace.	
WEDNESDAY	
OFF	WEIGHTS + RUNNING: Weights: You need to follow the exercises of the routine2. Execute 15 repetitions per exercise and switcht to the next exercise, and repeat the routine 1 3 times. Really short rest between exercises. This time, run 30' nice and easy after the weights, the first 10' at 9'00"pace OFF
THURSDAY	
SWIMMING : 2000y. Nice and easy. No longer than 50'	
FRIDAY	
RUNNING: 1h 1h. Easy run at 10'00" pace.	
SATURDAY	
BIKING + RUNNING (SESSION 1): 3h +35' Team (2 cyvlist) time trial + 35' track workout.	
SUNDAY	
OFF	TOTAL TIME: 6:40'

NOTES:
1.- Rest week. Perfect!, you can enjoy your short vacations ;-).
2.-Saturday is a key workout, It would be great if you can do it with us.

WEEK NUM. 10 FROM JULY 4 TO 10 2.005:

MONDAY
OFF
TUESDAY
RUNNING: 1h 50' 1h. 50' Easy run at 10'00" pace.
WEDNESDAY
OFF
THURSDAY
SWIMMING : 2000y. Nice and easy. No longer than 50'
FRIDAY
RUNNING: 1h 1h. Easy run at 10'00" pace.
SATURDAY
BIKING + RUNNING (SESSION 2): 2h + 5K *Tempo ride for 25miles + right after 5k. 5k in 26:30

SUNDAY	
SWIMMING : 2000y. Nice and easy. No longer than 50'	TOTAL TIME: 7:10'

NOTES:
1.- We are going to take this week easy, till you recover and feel better. You can skip any day except Saturday that will be a test for next Sunday.
2.- Saturday (all out), is the key workout. Get a loop of 25miles, and try to ride them as hard as possible, with only 1 or 2 stops, for water, and traffic lights . It is very important you try your best to go as fast as possible, and time it, becouse it would give me an idea how fast you can compete next Sunday, and we will be able to plan accordingly.

WEEK NUM. 11 FROM JULY 11 TO 17 2.005:

MONDAY
OFF
TUESDAY
RUNNING: 50' Nice and easy 50' run, to stretch out your legs.
WEDNESDAY
BIKING: 2h30 with specific bike workout. Ride part of the race length + S.B.W : W.U + 1 mile really fast + 10' easy + 2 miles really fast + 15' easy + 3 miles fast + Cool down till 2h.
THURSDAY
SWIMMING: 45' Nice and easy the entired swim length twice
FRIDAY
OFF
SATURDAY
TRIATHLON RACE Total time: 2h43'45"
SUNDAY

RUNNING + SWIMMING: 45'+ 45' Nice and easy 45' run, to stretch out your legs.+ 45' easy swim.	TOTAL TIME: 6:50'+ RACE

NOTES:
1.- Do as much as you can of this schedule, and feel confidence, becouse you are going to do a awesome job this comming Saturday.

Sprint distance triathlon

8 WEEKS TRAINING FOR A SUB 1H.
SPRINT DISTANCE TRIATHLON:

Athlete: John Kral (Male)
Age: 27
Weight: 160lbs
Profesion: Pro. Triathlete.
Base training prior to the program: 2 month 20 to 25 week
Time available for training: Every day, conditioned by work.
Groups: Master swimming group, cycling group, running partner.
Goal for the seasson: Top fininshings in Olympic and Sprint triathlons.

WEEK NUM.1 FROM SEPTEMBER 13 TO 19 MARCH 14 TO 20 2.008 (Specific training for Sprint)

MONDAY
OFF

TUESDAY

RUNNING + BIKING: 45'. nice and easy run (140bpm max) +
S.T 1
30' wu +
2 x 2' (1'easy)
2 x 3' (1'easy) all of them at 25miles/h
2 x 4' (1'easy)
2 x 5' + 30' Cool Down

WEDNESDAY

WEIGHTS + RUNNING: Follow the weights workout "routine 1". Repeat the whole workout 3 times. Right after 30' run at 6'24"/mile.	SWIMMING: 2.500m. Time to push. Intensity: 97% of your max HR. Work out 1: W.U 500m easy + 5 x 100m in 1' 10" (recovering 1full min. in between intervals + 100m nice and easy between sets)	
	6 x 75m in 50"	6 x 25" in 15"or less
	6 x 50m in 32"	Cool down 300m

THURSDAY

OFF

FRIDAY

BIKING + TRACK: 1h 45' at 20 miles/h average (included w.u)
+ Track

1 x 1.600m in 5'32" to 5'44"	1 x 800m in 2:30" to 2'35"
1 x 1.200m in 4'00" to 4'10"	1 x 400m in 1'10" to 1'12"
1 x 200m in 30" to 34' (rest: as long as you need to make the times)	

SATURDAY

BIKING + RUNNING:
2h30 nice and easy biking (135bpm max)
+ 25' nice and easy run (140bpm max)

SUNDAY

SWIMMING: 1h45' 5.000m. easy, easy pace. Long sets, anywhere between 300m and 500m. RUNNING: 1h10' 1h10' Tempo pace = 6'24" x mile	TOTAL: 13h15'

NOTES:
1.- Ok, we have to change our philosophy, quality& rest versus quantity. Your training will be mostly at midle-high intensity, get use to it.. They will be shorter and you have an extra day off a week, to make sure you recover properly from the speed workouts.

WEEK NUM. 2 FROM SEPTEMBER 20 TO 26
2.008 (Specific training for Sprint)

MONDAY	
OFF	

TUESDAY	
RUNNING + BIKING: 45'. nice and easy run (140bpm max) + S.T 2 30' wu +	2 x 4' (3'easy) 2 x 5' (3'easy) all of them at 25 miles/h 2 x 6' (3'easy) 2 x 7' + 30' Cool Down

WEDNESDAY	
WEIGHTS + RUNNING: Follow the weights workout "routine 2". Repeat the whole workout 3 times. Right after 35' easy run	SWIMMING: 1h. NICE AND EASY!! 3.000m. Work out 4: W.U 500m + + 4 x 500m easy = 5 (75 free+25stroke) 500m Cool down

THURSDAY
OFF

FRIDAY

BIKING + TRACK:
1h 45' at 20 miles/h average (included w.u)
+ Track

1 x 1.600m in 5'32"	1 x 1.600m in 5'40"	1 x 1.600m in 5'44"
1 x 200m in 32"	1 x 200m in 34"	1 x 200m in 36"

(rest: as long as you need to make the times)

SATURDAY

BIKING + RUNNING:
2h30 nice and easy biking (135bpm max)
+ 25' nice and easy run (140bpm max)

SUNDAY	
SWIMMING + BIKING + RUNNING : (Brick 4) Swimming 300m easy + 10km on the bike easy + 2k run in 6'30"!!+ (10'rest in between sets) Swimming 300m in 3'45" + 10km on the bike easy + 2k run easy. Swimming 300m 3'45" + 10km on the bike at 36km/h average + 2k run in 6'30"!! Cool down 10'	TOTAL: 14h10'

NOTES:
1.- Tuesday biking: Each time you go for an interval reset your computer and try to get at least 25miles/hour average.
2.-Track workouts. See if you can find some one to run with those days (it is better mentaly), may be Katia?

WEEK NUM. 3 FROM SEPTEMBER 27 TO 3
2.008 (Specific training for Sprint):

MONDAY	
OFF	

TUESDAY	
RUNNING: 50' run at 6'24"/mile	SWIMMING: 2000m. 200 warm up + 150m buterfly easy (20" recovering) + 100m IM kick super fast!(10" recovering) + 150m buterfly easy (20" recovering) + 1 x 400m Pull and padles (30" recovering) + 1 x 400 free (20" recovering) + 100m IM kick super fast!(20" recovering) + 100m breast easy (30" R) + 200m free Pull and padles (10"recovering) + 100m IM kick super fast!(20" recovering) + Cool down 100m

WEDNESDAY
BIKING + TRACK: 3h.30' or 56 miles Nice and easy biking up to only 155bpm TRACK: 20 x 200m in 32" (rest as long as you need to repeat the interval at the same pace)

THURSDAY	

OFF	SWIMMING: 2.350m. Everything easy.
	500 warm up +
	Drills: (everything with padles)
	X 1 x 200 free (30" recovering)
	4 x 50 (From now on called single arm stroke)
	  On the
	way down (25m) only stroke with your left arm,
	  on the way back with the right arm.
	200 free catch up (30" recovering) +
	400 IM kick fast only (1' recovering) +
	4 x 50 single arm stroke
	200m breathing every 2 strokes, 3, 5,7,9, and
	  again every 2,.....
	100m "touch your shoulder drill"
	Cool down 200m

FRIDAY
BIKING + RUNNING : 3h30' or 56 miles + 30' biking nice and easy (up to 155bpm) Right after, 30' run at 6'25"/mile.

SATURDAY
BIKING: 87 miles Long bike ride easy (up to 155bpm)

SUNDAY	
WEIGHTS + RUNNING: Weights for legs, abbdominals and low back. w.u 10' treadmil 3 sets of 15 reps. of leg extension leg press seat ups leg curl Calf rises low back exercises All of it with 1' rest in between sets and exercises. Right after 35' run at 6'25"/mile.	TOTAL TIME: 16:30' hours

NOTES:

1.- Tuesday. Track workout needs to be right after the bike. So leave the bike on the track and start right away the first interval of 200m. Rest as much as you need to mantain the pace. It doesn't work to do them slower with less rest.

2.- The rest of the week it is easy, with the exception of the weights ☺

3.- I can do some of the workouts with you this week.

WEEK NUM. 4 FROM OCTOBER 4 TO 10 2.008:

MONDAY
OFF

TUESDAY
BIKING + TRACK: 3h.30' or 56 miles Nice and easy biking up to only 155bpm TRACK : 15 x 400m in 1'10" TO 1'18" (rest as long as you need to repeat the interval at the same pace)

WEDNESDAY	
RUNNING: 55' Steady run 6'24" to 6'36" x mile.	SWIMMING: 2.500m 300 warm up styles + 4 x 400 free in 5' with 30" R 1 x 400 IM kick + Cool down 200m

THURSDAY
RUNNING + BIKING: 30' + 3h30' or 56 miles 30' Steady run 6'24" to 6'36" x mile Right after, biking nice and easy (up to 155bpm)

FRIDAY
WEIGHTS + RUNNING: Weights for legs, abbdominals and low back. w.u 10' treadmil 3 sets of 15 reps. of leg extension " " leg curl " " leg press " " Calf rises " " seat ups " " low back exercises All of it with 1' rest in between sets and exercises. Right after 35' at tempo run = 6'8" to 6'24" x mile

SATURDAY	
BIKING: 87 miles Long bike ride easy (up to 155bpm)	SWIMMING: 2.500m. easy. 200 warm up + 300m buterfly easy (1' recovering) + 200m IM kick super fast!(30" recovering) + 200m = (75 buterfly easy+ 25 other stroke)1' recovering + 1 x 400m Pull and padles (1' recovering) = 25 fast /75 easy + 50 fast/50easy + 75fast/25esy + 100fast 200m IM(1 R) + 100m IM (30" R) + 50m IM (30"R) + 1 x 400 free (30" R) + 1 x 400 = 25 buter/75 back + 50 brest/50free + 75buter/25back + 100brest (1' R) + 100m IM kick super fast!(30" recovering) + Cool down 100m

SUNDAY	
RUNNING: 1h.30" Long run. (Steady run 6'24" to 6'36"/ mile)	TOTAL TIME: 20:00 hours

NOTES:

1.- Steady running pace up to 155 + or - . The Tempo run 162 bpm + or - .

2.- The track workout is going to be more specific, longer and harder, and needs to be right after the bike, so leave the bike on the track and without warm up start doing the intervals.

3.- From now on your goal will be rest and recover as much as possible in between days and workouts. That means : 9hours of sleep a day, lots of drinks, lots of healthy foot (prohibit any form of junk food).

4.- And mostly, I need in the next reports you send me you tell me how you feel, and how high is your energy. If you feel too tired or you are recovering fast enough.

WEEK NUM. 5 FROM OCTOBER 11 TO 17 2.008:

MONDAY	
OFF	
TUESDAY	
BIKING + TRACK: 2:30'h. or 56 miles Nice and easy biking up to only 155bpm TRACK WORKOUT: 8 x 800m in 2'30" TO 2'36" (rest as long as you need to repeat the interval at the same pace!!!)	
WEDNESDAY	
WEIGHTS + RUNNING: Follow the weights workout "rutine 1" Right after 50' at tempo run = 6'8" to 6'24" x mile	SWIMMING: 2.750m. Intervals. All out!! 500 warm up + 1 x 500 free (1' R) + 1 x 250m free (1' R) + 1 x 200 IM kick (1' R) + 1 x 100m IM (30" R) + 1 x 50m back sprint (30" R) + 1 x 200 IM kick (1' R) + 1 x 100m IM (30" R) + 1 x 250m free (1' R) + 1 x 500 free (2' R) + Cool down 100m
THURSDAY	
OFF	SWIMMING: 2.000m 500 warm up broken + 5 x 150m 1.- 25 l. Arm + 25 r. arm + 50 regular +50 kick 2.- 25 breast with free kick + 25 with dolfin kick + 50 regular + 50 kick 3.- 50 free catch up + 50 touch shoulder + 50 kick 4.- 100 back + 50 back kick 5.- free breathing every 2, 3, 4, 5, 6, 7, 8, 9, 2, ... 3 x 200 free 1.- Fast free 2.- Fast breast 3.- Fast back Cool Down 150m
FRIDAY	
RUNNING + BIKING: 40' + 2h 40' Steady run 6'24" to 6'36" x mile Right after, bike time trial (1)	
SATURDAY	
RUNNING: 1h.30" Long run. (up to 140bpm)	SWIMMING: 2.000m Easy. 500 warm up + Drills: 5 x 100 free catch up (30" R) + 6 x 50 On the way down (25m) only stroke with your left arm, on the way back with the right arm. 3 x 100m "touch your shoulder drill" 1 x 200 IM kick super fast! (1' R) + 1 x 200m Pull and padles = 3 length easy 1 super fast (20" R) + Cool down 100m
SUNDAY	
BIKING: 70 miles Long bike ride easy (up to 155bpm)	TOTAL TIME: 16:45' hours

NOTES:

1.- Weights: I send you a workout I want you do. It is general for all your body, but I really want you push as hard as possible on the legs exercises!!! You want them heavy, heavy, heavy!!!!

2.- The track workout is going to be more specific, and harder. This time rest more than 90" if you need it.

3.- Rest is really important mostly when you do so much speed workout.

4.- Bike time trial: Ok, here is what you do: Run the 40' at 6'24" to 6' 36" pace, right after take the bike and start the time trial. Two full loops of 10 miles. No drafting alowed + 10' cool down.

5.- Sunday massage! ;)

WEEK NUM. 6 FROM OCTOBER 18 TO 24 2.008:

MONDAY
OFF

TUESDAY
BIKING + TRACK: 2:30'h. or 50 miles Nice and easy biking up to only 155bpm TRACK: 4 x 1.600m in 5'45" TO 5'55" (rest as long as you need to repeat the interval at the same pace!!!)

WEDNESDAY	
RUNNING: 45' Steady run 6'24" to 6'36" x mile.	SWIMMING: 2.650m Fast!. 500 warm up + Set 1: 2 X 350m = 100m free easy + 50m back sprint +50 free kick + 50 breast easy + 100 free easy (1' R " ") Set 2: 2 X 700 = 300m Pull and Padles + 50 breast + 100m free + 50 breast kick + 200 free fast (1' R end of the interval) Set 3: 2 X 550m = 100 back fast + 100 free easy + 50 free kick sprint + 100 back + 100 free kick fast (1' recovering " ") + Cool down 300m

THURSDAY
RUNNING + BIKING: 45' + 2h or 40 miles 30' Steady run 6'24" to 6'36" x mile Right after, biking nice and easy (up to 155bpm)

FRIDAY	
WEIGHTS + RUNNING: Follow the weights workout "rutine 1". Repeat the whole workout 3 times. Right after 30' at tempo run = 6'8" to 6'24" x mile	SWIMMING: 2.000m Fast!. 500m W.U + 1000m in 12'(test) + 500m Cool down.

SATURDAY
RUNNING: 1h.30" Long run. (up to 140bpm)

SUNDAY	
BIKING: 2h30' about 50 miles Bike time trial (2)	SWIMMING: 2.650m Easy 500 warm up + Set 1: 4 X 100m free(10"R) + 100m IM kick fast Set 2: 5 X 200m free (20"R) + 100m IM kick Set 3: 4 X 100m free (20"R) + 100m IM kick Cool down 300m TOTAL TIME: 19:15 hours

NOTES:
1.- There are 3 really important workouts you need to really push. Tuesday track , Friday weights and Sunday bike time trial. It is therefore really important to make them at hieghest intensity. As you can see, you train less hours so you can recover from the Speed workouts.
2.- Sunday. We will leave from my house nice and easy till "the loop" ☺ (20 miles), and we will do an individual time trial to the whole loop (to the traffic light). The goal here is to get at least an average speed of 25 miles/h. We will leave every 45" seconds apart.
3.- The track workout is increasing in distance every week. Leave the bike on the track and without warm up start doing the intervals.
4.- If you aren't working out, rest, rest, rest.

229

Carlos Civit

WEEK NUM. 7 FROM OCTOBER 25 TO 31 2.008:

MONDAY	
OFF	
TUESDAY	
RUNNING: 45' Nice and easy (up to 140bpm max).	SWIMMING: (my favorite workout!!!) 500m warm up + 12 x 100m free = 100m in 1'35" + 100m in 1'30" + 100m in 1'15" + 100m in 1'25" + 100m in 1'20" + 100m in 1'20" + 100m in 1'25" + 100m in 1'15" + 100m in 1'30" + 100m in 1'10" + 100m in 1'35" + 100m in 1'10" + Cool down = 100 IM kick really easy.
WEDNESDAY	
BIKING + TRACK: 2:30'h. or 50 miles Nice and easy biking up to only 155bpm	TRACK : 3 x 2.000m in 6'30" TO 6'40" (rest as long as you need to repeat the interval at the same pace!!!)
THURSDAY	
OFF	OPEN WATER SWIM: 1h. Nice and easy swim in the sea, trying to breath by both sides.
FRIDAY	
RUNNING: 45' Nice and easy (up to 140bpm max).	SWIMMING: Easy. 500 warm up + Set 1: 300 Pull and Padles (1' R) + 2 x 100m 2 X (25m right arm 25 m left arm) 15"R + 300m free(1'R) + 2 x 100 Catch up (15"R) 300 Pull and Padles (1' R) + 2 x 100m IM kick fast Set 2: 5 X 100m free = 1.- Free with the 3rd length sprint (15") 2.- Back with 2nd length sprint (15") 3,- Breast with the fst length sprint 4.- Free fast 5.- Free fast. (15") + 200m IM kick Set 3: 200m Pull and Padles (30"R) + 200m IM kick Cool down 100m
SATURDAY	
RUNNING + BIKING: 30' + 2h 30' 30' Steady run 6'24" to 6'36" x mile Right after, Bike time trial (3)	
SUNDAY	
RUNNING: 1h15'Nice and easy run (up to 140bpm)	TOTAL TIME: 12:00 hours

NOTES:

1.- First tapering week. You just have two really hard workouts, Wednesday and Saturday, the rest of the week is just to recover as much as possible. Now, those 2 workouts need to be done at your highest level.

2.- Saturday: We will repeat exactly the same workout than last Saturday. The goal here is to get at least an average speed of 25 miles/h. No excuses!. We will leave every 45" seconds apart.

3.- No weights this week.

4.- The track workout is longer and harder. Leave the bike on the track and without warm up start doing the intervals.

WEEK NUM. 8 FROM NOVEMBER 1 TO 7 2.008:

MONDAY
OFF

TUESDAY
BIKING: 1h up to 2h. It depends how you feel that day. Intensity: Low, up to 150bpm.

WEDNESDAY	
RUNNING: 45' Nice and easy (up to 140bpm max).	OPEN WATER SWIM: 1h. Nice and easy swim in the sea, trying to breath by both sides.

THURSDAY
BIKING + RUNNING: 1h easy (up to 155bpm) + right after 25' steady run 6:20 to 6:30 x mile.

FRIDAY	
OFF	OPEN WATER SWIM: 1h. Nice and easy swim in the sea, trying to breath by both sides.

SATURDAY
RUNNING + BIKING: 15' + 30' Intensity: Easy running + Easy biking

SUNDAY	
DUATHLON:	TOTAL TIME: 5h25' + Race.

NOTES:
1.- Second tapering week. No Hard workouts at all. Rest, rest, rest.
2.- Tuesday: You need to be honest with yourself, and ride what you feel more confortable, it could be 1h. Up to 2h. But no more. Always easy though.
3.- No weights this week.
4.- Sunday: Test competition. Just go at 90% of you max, just enough to get the racing mentallity on again. Remember the big day is next Saturday.

WEEK NUM. 9 FROM NOVEMBER 8 TO 14 2.008:

MONDAY	
OFF	
TUESDAY	
RUNNING: 45' Nice and easy (up to 140bpm max).	OPEN WATER SWIM: 1h. Nice and easy swim in the sea, trying to breath by both sides.
WEDNESDAY	
OFF	
THURSDAY	
RUNNING: 45' Nice and easy (up to 140bpm max).	
FRIDAY	
RUNNING: 35' Nice and easy (up to 140bpm max).	OPEN WATER SWIM: 30' Nice and easy swim in the sea, trying to breath by both sides.
SATURDAY	
SPRINT TRIATHLON: Total time: 1h. 55'	
SUNDAY	
OFF	TOTAL TIME: 3h35' + Race.

NOTES:
1.- As you can see easy week, and it has to be that way.

8 WEEKS TRAINING FOR A 1h.5' TO 15' SPRINT DISTANCE TRIATHLON:

Athlete: Lacy Utterback (Female)
Age: 30
Weight: 125lbs
Profesion: Psycologist
Base training prior to the program: 10 week
Time available for training: Every day, conditioned by work.
Groups: Master swimming group, cycling group.
Goal for the seasson: Her first seasson in the sport of triathlon.

WEEK NUM. 1 FROM JANUARY 5 TO 11 2.004:

MONDAY
SPINNING : 1h. Spinning with Carles Civit at 6:55pm Intensity: High. Up to 180bpm.

TUESDAY
SWIMMING: 1h. Master swimming with Chris at 5:30pm. or also you can go by yourself. Intensity: Moderate. Up to 163bpm.

WEDNESDAY	
RUNNING: 1h. Intensity high up to 172rpm. Workout: 20' warm up + 20' farlek on the streets (one stretch walkside sprinting, next one really easy, next sprinting again, ...till you make the 20'), + 20' cool down. On the tread mill (better no): 20' warm up + 1' fast 1' easy till you get the 20' (everything wth inclination of 9%) + 20' cool down.	OPTION 2: 1h aquajogging. In case your foot still hurts you may do what is called aquajogging. In the aquatics department can show you how to do it.

THURSDAY
SPINNING:1h. Spinning with Carles at 6:00pm. Intensity: Moderate. Up to 165bpm.

FRIDAY	
RUNNING: 45' Nice and easy run for 45'.	OPTION 2: Pilates Pilates at 9:35am with June.

SATURDAY
BRICK 3: 2h. 1 hour spinning with Johanna. Intensity: low. Up to 154bpm. + 1hour running. Intensity: medium. Up to 168bpm. (if it is possible try to run the first 5' as hard as possible, and then slow down).

SUNDAY	
HIKE or RUN: Hike: Up to 2 hours. (155 HR Max) or 1h30' run(150 HR Max)	TOTAL TIME: 8:15'

NOTES:
1.- Wednesday: On this day you have two options, it is better if you take the one on the streets. That workout is one I used to do in Barcelona when I couldn't do track or I just was to sick of it. Consist in run as fast as possible from one intersection to another, and then easy to the next one, and then fast again, and on, and on. Call me if you have any doubts.
2.- Saturday: Brick. Each week we will train a different brick, and different intensities. This week spinning + running.

WEEK NUM. 2 FROM JANUARY 12 TO 18 2.004:

MONDAY
SPINNING : 1h. Spinning with Carles Civit at 6:55pm Intensity: Moderate
TUESDAY
TRACK: 1h. 8 X 400m in 1'35" Track workout. same place same hour than always. Intensity: High. Up to 180bpm.
WEDNESDAY
RUNNING: 1h. Nice and easy run. Intensity low up to 155rpm.
THURSDAY
SPINNING:1h. Spinning with Carles at 6:00pm. Intensity: Moderate. Up to 165bpm.
FRIDAY
SWIMMING: 1h. Master's swimming. Intensity: Moderate to high. (it depends how you feel).
SATURDAY
BRICK 4: 2h. 1 hour 30' on a road bike + 5' transition + 30' run.. Intensity: low. Up to 154bpm. on the bike Moderate on the run up to 162rpm
SUNDAY

HIKE or RUN:	
Hike: Up to 2 hours. (155 HR Max) or 1h30' run(150 HR Max)	TOTAL TIME: 8:15'

NOTES:
1.- Tuesday: It would be good you can run on the track.
2.- Friday: From now on you aren't going to swim so much, therefore is better to push a litle bit on the days you do.
3.- Saturday: real road bike! :) and then try to run a litle bit high intensity on your run. Since is going to be your first brick since a while a go, just running at a litle bit unconfortable pace it would be enough.

WEEK NUM. 3 FROM JANUARY 12 TO 18 2.004:

MONDAY
SPINNING : 1h. Spinning with Carles Civit at 6:55pm Intensity: Hard!! Up to 172bpm.

TUESDAY	
OFF	TRACK: OFF

WEDNESDAY
RUNNING: 1h. Nice and easy run. with 10' at fast pace. Intensity moderate up to 162rpm. during 50' of the workout. High intensity for the 10'   interval.

THURSDAY
MINI-BRICK:1h. 45' Spinning +15' fast run. Intensity: Spinning: Moderate. Up to 165bpm. Running: high. Up to 172.

FRIDAY
SWIMMING: 1h. Master's swimming. Intensity: low .

SATURDAY
BRICK 4: 2h.20' 1 hour 45' on a road bike + 5' transition + 35' run.. Intensity: low. Up to 154bpm. on the bike Moderate on the run up to 162rpm (so far no hurries with transitions)

SUNDAY	
HIKE or RUN or SWIM and RUN: Hike: Up to 2 hours. (155 HR Max) or 1h30' run(150 HR Max) or 1hour swimming with master's and 45' run.	TOTAL TIME: 7:50'

NOTES:
1.- Tuesday: Off.
2.- Thursday: Mini-brick. Leave your running shoes outside of the spinning room, and spinning for 45' and then cheange your shoes as fast as posssible and run for 15' at a fast tempo run.
3.- This week as you can see the overall intensity is higher, but it is really important that you try to follow the intensities I ask you. I know that some times could seem really hard, but at least try it.
4.-Sunday: Whatever you chouse but take it easy.

WEEK NUM. 4 FROM FABRUARY 2 TO 8 2.004:

MONDAY
SPINNING : 1h. Spinning with Carles Civit at 6:55pm Intensity: Hard!! Up to 172bpm.

TUESDAY	
WEIGHTS + RUNNING: (brick) Weights for legs + 45' run Intensity: Hard for the legs session/ easy for the running	TRACK: OFF

WEDNESDAY
SWIMMING: 1h. Master's swimming. Intensity: low up to moderate.

THURSDAY
MINI-BRICK:1h 10'. 45' Spinning +20' fast run + 5' cool down. Intensity: Spinning: easy. Up to 155bpm. Running: high. Up to 172!!.

FRIDAY
RUNNING: 1h. Nice and easy run. Intensity: low .

SATURDAY
RUNNING: 30' 30' nice and easy run.

SUNDAY	
SAN DIEGUITO 5K RUN	TOTAL TIME: 6:30'

NOTES:
1.- This week you have less hours of training, becouse I want you be rested for Sunday race. I really want you give everything you have. No excusses!
2.- Tuesday: Try to do both sessions back to back.
3.- Thursday: Mini-brick. It is really important this Thursday that you run the 20' as hard as possible. You need this speed workout in order to be ready for Sunday race. Leave your running shoes outside of the spinning room.
4.-Saturday: It is going to be yopur day almost OFF. So just run 30' really easy.
5.-Sunday: Your first race this seasson. Push as hard as possible!! You can do it well. Don't be conservative and give everything you have.

WEEK NUM. 5 FROM FABRUARY 9 TO 15 2.004:

MONDAY
SPINNING : 1h. Spinning with Carles Civit at 6:55pm Intensity: low! Up to 145bpm.

TUESDAY	
WEIGHTS + RUNNING: (brick) OFF	TRACK: OFF

WEDNESDAY
SWIMMING: 1h. Master's swimming with Carles. Intensity: moderate up to 162.

THURSDAY
MINI-BRICK:1h 20'. Full spin class +15' fast run* + 5' cool down. Intensity: Spinning: easy. Up to 155bpm. Running: high. Up to 172!!. *Run workout: 10x (30"almost sprint +1' easy) = 15'run

FRIDAY
SWIMMING: 1h. Master's swimming with carles. Intensity: high

SATURDAY
BRICK6: 2h30' 1h50' on a road bike + 5'transition + 40' run. Intensity: low. Up to 154bpm on the bike moderate on the run, up to 162bpm. (easy transitions)

SUNDAY	
HIKE OR MINI-BRICK: Hike: Up to 2hours. MINI-BRICK: 20'swim + 20'spinning + 20'run (intensity no less than moderate)	TOTAL TIME: 7:50'

NOTES:
1.- Monday: Use this day to recover from the race.
2.-Saturday: Is your long session of the week.
3.- Sunday: If you are going to do the mini-brick, try to make it at a
    good tempo pace, preatty close to your race goal pace = 900y in
    the 20', 2.5 miles for the 20'run.

WEEK NUM. 6 FROM FABRUARY 23 TO 29 2.004:

MONDAY
SWIMMING: 1h. Master swimmimg from 8 to 9:15am Intensity: low! Up to 155bpm. Just to let you recover your legs.
TUESDAY
TRACK: Track at La Costa Canyon High Schol. At 5:30pm. Intensity: High = race pace goal.
WEDNESDAY
1fr. MINI-TRIATHLON TEST: 1h.10' Swimming for 20' + spinning for 35' + running for 15' Intensities: S. Moderate + S. Easy + R. Hard
THURSDAY
SPINNING:1h Full spin class with Carles Civit at 6:00pm. Intensity: Low up to 155bpm
FRIDAY
SWIMMING + RUNNING: 30' + 45'. Master's swimming with carles for 30'.+ 45' run Intensity: high + low
SATURDAY
BRICK6: 2h45' 2h on a road bike + 5'transition + 45' run. Intensity: low. Up to 154bpm on the bike moderate on the run, up to 162bpm. (easy transitions)
SUNDAY

HIKE OR MINI-BRICK: Hike: Up to 2hours. MINI-BRICK: 40'swim + 1h spinning (intensity no less than moderate)	TOTAL TIME: up to 10:10'

NOTES:
1.- Well, since you are rested, this week we'll increase the volume a litle bit. Remember, we are almost at your race seasson.
2.- Tuesday: We incorporate track workout again. You need that kind of intensity.
3.- Saturday: Is your long session of the week. This week even longer, but these workouts give you the endurance you need to handle the speed workout.
5.- Sunday: You have two options. Bouth are good.

WEEK NUM. 7 FROM MARCH 1 TO 7 2.004:

MONDAY
SWIMMING: 1h. Master swimmimg from 8 to 9:15am Intensity: low! Up to 155bpm. Just to let you recover your legs.

TUESDAY
1fr. MINI-TRIATHLON TEST: 1h.10' Swimming for 20' + spinning for 35' + running for 15' Intensities: S. Moderate + S. Easy + R. Hard

WEDNESDAY
WEIGHTS: 1h. Heavy weights for 1h. with me.

THURSDAY
SPINNING:1h Full spin class with Carles Civit at 6:00pm. Intensity: Low up to 155bpm

FRIDAY	
RUN: 1h. Nice and easy run + 10 x 100yards accelerations up to sprint. Intensity: Low 155bpm on the easy run High on the sprints.	(Option 2) SWIMMING: 1h. Master swimming from 8 to 9:15am Intensity: low! Up to 155bpm.

SATURDAY	
BRICK6: 2h55 2h 30'on a road bike + 5'transition + 25' run. Intensity: low. Up to 154bpm on the bike moderate on the run, up to 162bpm. (easy transitions)	

SUNDAY	
HIKE OR MINI-BRICK: Hike: Up to 2hours. MINI-BRICK: 1hswim + 1h spinning (intensity no less than moderate)	TOTAL TIME: up to 9:55'

NOTES:
1.- Tuesday: No track workout! You will do the mini-triathlon test
    again, (since you didin't do it last week.
3.- Friday: Two options again.
4.- Sunday: You have two options. Bouth are good.

WEEK NUM. 8 FROM MARCH 8 TO 14 2.004:

MONDAY
SPINNING + SWIMMING: 1h 45'
Spinning at 6:55am
Master swimmimg from 8 to 9:15am
Intensity: low! Up to 155bpm. on the bike, moderate in the pool.

TUESDAY
RUN: 1h.
1h. nice and easy with 2 loops to the track (Torrey Pines track in 3'30") +cool down back home.

WEDNESDAY
OFF

THURSDAY
SPINNING:1h
Full spin class with Carles Civit at 6:00pm.
Intensity: High up to 175bpm

FRIDAY
1fr. MINI-TRIATHLON TEST: 1h.10'
Spinning for 45' + running for 20' + swimming for 25'
Intensities: S. Hard + R. Easy + S. easy

SATURDAY
35' nice and easy run

SUNDAY	
TEMECULA SPRINT TRIATHLON Total time: 10'10" + 55'27" + 27'53" = 1h11'	TOTAL TIME: up to 7:00' or 9:00

NOTES:
1.- Tuesday: You have a run plus 2 loops to Torrey Pines track. Please do them.
2.- Triathlon race = All out!!

10 WEEKS TRAINING FOR A JUST FINISH SPRINT DISTANCE TRIATHLON:

Athlete: Cari Blury (Female)
Age: 40
Weight: 135lbs
Profesion: Sales representative.
Base training prior to the program: Spinning and running 3 to 4 days a week.
Time available for training: Every day, conditioned by work.
Groups: Master swimming masters, turbo training organize workout, rest alone.
Goal for the seasson: Just finish her first triathlon..

WEEK NUM. 1 FROM JANUARY 5 TO 11 2.004:

MONDAY	
OFF	
TUESDAY	
BIKE: 1h 35' Total. Nice and easy ride,	
WEDNESDAY	
MASTERS' SWIM: Easy	TURBO TRAINING: Whatever Terry ask you. Intensity: Moderate. Up to 75%
THURSDAY	
WEIGHTS + RUN: Weights for upperbody + run 30' (last 5' before the cool down hard!)	
FRIDAY	
MASTERS' SWIM: Whatever they ask you. Intensity: moderate up tp 75%	AFTERNOON: OFF
SATURDAY	
BRICK 2h workout: 1h 30'bike + 30' run This week: BIKE easy + RUN fast! Slow transition if you want.	
SUNDAY	
RUN: 1h5' run easy	TOTAL TIME: 9:40'

> **NOTES:**
> 1.- As you can see you have a bunch of hours this week. Overall intensity is still low, but with some fast workouts. Let's see if it feels good or it make you feel too tired. We need to be really careful these first weeks.
> 2.- If for any reason you feel too tired to start any workout, leave.

WEEK NUM. 2 FROM JANUARY 12 TO 18 2.004:

MONDAY	
OFF	
TUESDAY	
BIKE: 1h 40' Total. Nice and easy ride,	
WEDNESDAY	
MASTERS' SWIM: 1h easy but I need you swim 500y at least at 1:45" per 100y.	TURBO TRAINING: Whatever Terry ask you. Intensity: Moderate. Up to 75%
THURSDAY	
WEIGHTS + RUN: Weights for legs + run 35' (last 10' before the cool down hard!)	
FRIDAY	
MASTERS' SWIM: Whatever they ask you. Intensity: moderate up to 75%	AFTERNOON: 45' nice and really easy run
SATURDAY	
BRICK 2h 10'workout: 1h 30'bike + 40' run This week: BIKE easy + RUN 1/2 fast 1/2 easy! Slow transition if you want.	
SUNDAY	
RUN: 1h10' run easy	TOTAL TIME: 10:30'

NOTES:
1.- Wednesday: From all the yards you swim you need to start swimming at race pace. So, so far on Wednesday from all your swimming, 500 yards (they don't need to be done straight or in the same set) needs to be done at 1'45" pace.
2.- Thusday: Weights can't take you longer than 1h.
3.- Saturday: The first part of the run try to go at race pace, then slow down and make it confortable.

WEEK NUM. 3 FROM FEBRUARY 2 TO 8 2.004:

MONDAY
OFF

TUESDAY
BIKE: Specific training (S.T) 1 W.U 20' nice and easy + 5 x (1' left leg + 1' right leg) + 10 x (1' spin with the shortest gear + 1' normal) + 55' nice and easy 1h 45' Total.

WEDNESDAY	
MASTERS' SWIM: 1h swim. Test 1: 5 x 100y. as fast as possible. 3' rest in between	TURBO TRAINING: Whatever Terry ask you. Intensity: Moderate. Up to 75%

THURSDAY
WEIGHTS + RUN: Weights for legs + run 45' with 10 x 50y up hill accelerations.

FRIDAY	
MASTERS' SWIM: OFF	AFTERNOON: OFF

SATURDAY
RUN: 40' Nice and easy with 5 x 50y up hill accelerations.

SUNDAY	
SAN DIEGUITO 5K & 1/2 MARATHON RACE.	TOTAL TIME: 7:55'

NOTES:
1.- Wednesday: I need you try to swim as hard as possible every single interval of thouse 5 x 100y, and keep track of them. Rest plenty in between (3' or more if you need it)
2.- This sunday your first race. You can chouse in between 5k and the 1/2 marathon. Eather one you need to give your best. That will give us an idea of your running fitness + wiil make you be used to the competition.

WEEK NUM. 4 FROM FEBRUARY 16 TO 22 2.004:

MONDAY	
OFF	
TUESDAY	

BIKE: Specific training (S.T) 3
W.U 20' nice and easy + 3 x (2' left leg + 2'
  right leg)
+ 4 x (1' left leg + 1' right leg)
+ 5 x (30" left leg + 30" right leg)
+ 3 x (15" left leg + 15" right leg)
+ 55' nice and easy
1h 45' Total.
	TRACK:
	1h. Track workout.
	From now on every tuesday we will run
	  together (with more people) at La Costa
	  Canyon High School track. We always
	  meet at 5:30pm. To run intervals.

WEDNESDAY	
MASTERS' SWIM: 1h swim. Intensity: Really easy	TURBO TRAINING: This week no
THURSDAY	
WEIGHTS + RUN: Weights for upper body + run 45'	
FRIDAY	
MASTERS' SWIM: OFF	AFTERNOON: OFF
SATURDAY	
RUN: 30' Nice and easy with 5 x 50y up hill accelerations.	
SUNDAY	
TORRY PINES 5K RUN	TOTAL TIME: 6:30'

NOTES:
1.- Tuesday: The ST3 needs to be done with the longest gear you can turn. It is a power exercise!
2.- This sunday your secon test- race, Torry Pines 5k run. You need to give your best. That will make you be used to the competition.
3.- W.U on the race day: 1hour before the race: Run nice and easy for 25' .Then rest and stretch for 20 more minutes. And finally 15' minutes before the start, run 5 accelerations of 50y. up hill, and make sure you have a good possition on the start line.

WEEK NUM. 5 FROM FEBRUARY 23 TO 29 2.004:

MONDAY	
OFF	
TUESDAY	
BIKE: 1h.30' Nice and easy 1h.30'	TRACK: No this week
WEDNESDAY	
MASTERS' SWIM: 1h swim. Intensity: Really easy	TURBO TRAINING: This week no
THURSDAY	
WEIGHTS + RUN: This week no.	RUN:1h. Nice and easy
FRIDAY	
MASTERS' SWIM: Whatever they ask you with a test (2nd)of 1.000yards in 18')	AFTERNOON: OFF
SATURDAY	
BRICK: 3h. On the bike + 7k. Running Intensity: Everything easy.	
SUNDAY	
RUN: **1h10' Nice and easy.**	TOTAL TIME: 6:10'

NOTES:
1.- This week: Everything

WEEK NUM. 6 FROM MARCH 1 TO 7 2.004:

MONDAY	
OFF	
TUESDAY	
TRACK: Warm Up + 1x 400m under 1'50" 200m walk. 600m under 3' 200m walk 1000m under 5' Cool down.	
WEDNESDAY	
MASTERS' SWIM: 1h swim. Intensity: Really easy	TURBO TRAINING: This week yes Intensity: Moderate.
THURSDAY	
BIKE: 1h.45'nice and easy, With 3 x (1'L.leg + 1' R.leg + 2' Hard) 5' n&e 6' at race pace = 18 miles per hour. Cool Down	
FRIDAY	
MASTERS' SWIM: Test of the 1.500y.	
SATURDAY	
BRICK: 3h. On the bike + 6 miles running Intensity: Everything easy.	
SUNDAY	
RUN: **1h15' Nice and easy. = 1 full hour of stretching**	TOTAL TIME: 11:30'

NOTES:
1.- This week: Some changes let me know if they fit to you. Tuesday: You have 2 options: Or my workout, or the workout they ask you. Both can be good.
2.- Friday: You have a test in the pool. It would be good if you can do it with someone else. And it is important you don't stop during the test.

WEEK NUM.7 FROM MARCH 8 TO 14 2.004:

MONDAY	
OFF	
TUESDAY	
BIKE: 1h.45'nice and easy, With 9' (45"L.leg + 45" R.leg) 5' n&e 3 X 1' with 53 x 16 gear 1' with 53 x 15 gear 1' with 53 x 14 gear 1' with 53 x 13 gear 1' with 53 x 13 gear standing up. Cool Down	TRACK: Warm Up + 6 x 1000m in 4'40" (400m jogging) + Cool down.
WEDNESDAY	
MASTERS' SWIM: 1h swim. Intensity: Really easy	TURBO TRAINING: This week NO
THURSDAY	
RUN: **45' Nice and easy. = 1 full hour of stretching**	
FRIDAY	
OFF	
SATURDAY	
BRICK: 1h. On the bike + 2 miles running Intensity: Everything easy.	
SUNDAY	
TEMECULA SPRINT TRIATHLON	TOTAL TIME: 7:20'

NOTES:
1.- This week: Some changes let me know if they fit to you.
2.- Tuesday: You have 2 options: Or my workout, or the workout they
   ask you, both can be good.
3.- Saturday. Still training but take it easy.
4.- Sunday. Temecula Sprint triathlon. Your first real test.

WEEK NUM. 8 FROM MARCH 15 TO 21 2.004:

MONDAY	
OFF	
TUESDAY	
RUN: **45' Nice and easy.**	TRACK: off
WEDNESDAY	
MASTERS' SWIM: Whatever they ask you. Intensity: Moderate.	TURBO TRAINING: OFF
THURSDAY	
BIKE: 1h.45'nice and easy, Todays workout: POWER!! With 10' (20"L.leg + 20" R.leg) with the longer gear you have. 5' n&e regular gear. 20' (30" sprint + 1'30" nice and easy) all them with the longest gear you have. Cool Down	
FRIDAY	
MASTERS' SWIM: Whatever they ask you. Intensity: Moderate	
SATURDAY	
BRICK: 2h.30'. On the bike + 2 miles running Intensity: On the bike at 70% On the run at 90%	
SUNDAY	
RUN: 1h.30' nice and easy run. Intensity: 65%	TOTAL TIME: 9:00'

NOTES:
1.- First 1/2 week will be for recovering from the race, both can be
    good.
2.- Sunday. You have a long run, but if you feel to tired or your knee
    is bodering you you can make it shorter.
3.- Saturday. Still training but take it easy.
4.- Sunday. Temecula Sprint triathlon. Your first real test.

WEEK NUM. 9 FROM MARCH 22 TO 28 2.004:

MONDAY	
OFF	
TUESDAY	
BIKE: 1h.45'nice and easy, With 9' (2' L.leg + 2' R.leg) 5' n&e 3 X 1'hard 1' easy 1' hard 1' easy 5' nice and easy between sets. Cool Down	TRACK: Warm Up + 2 x 3000m in 14' 30" (800m jogging) + Cool down.
WEDNESDAY	
MASTERS' SWIM: 1h swim. Intensity: Really easy	TURBO TRAINING: This week yes!
THURSDAY	
RUN: **35' Nice and easy. = 1 full hour of stretching**	
FRIDAY	
MASTERS' SWIM: 1h swim. Intensity: Really easy	
SATURDAY	
BRICK: 3h35' 3h. On the bike + 7k. Running Intensity: Everything easy.	
SUNDAY	
RUN: **1h15' Nice and easy.**	TOTAL TIME: 10:10'

NOTES:
1.- This week: More hours and hardesr :).
2.- Tuesday: the hardest day
3.- Saturday. If you don't have anyone to go with, I have a friend that she is at your same level that could join you. Let me know.
4.- Sunday. The pace needs to be really easy.

WEEK NUM. 10 FROM MARCH 29 TO 4 2.004:

MONDAY	
OFF	
TUESDAY	
TRACK: (Specific workout for California) w.u 10' + 2 x 1.600m in 5'45". 400m rest in between. + Cool down.	
WEDNESDAY	
MASTERS' SWIM: Only 45'!!! Whatever they ask you. (but from now on 90% of the workout needs to be freestyle) Intensity: Easy (H.R Max 155b.p.m)	TURBO TRAINING: No this week.
THURSDAY	
OFF	
FRIDAY	
35' n&e bike ride + 25' nice and easy run	
SATURDAY	
SPRINT TRIATHLON: Total time = 1h.45'	
SUNDAY	
OFF	TOTAL: UP TO 2:45' + RACE

NOTES:
1.- There is nothing else to do but resting.
2.- Thursday. The biking must be done with your road bike.

CPSIA information can be obtained at www.ICGtesting.com
Printed in the USA
BVOW041012021211

277295BV00002B/321/P

9 781456 722999